a popular guide
to new testament criticism

a popular guide
to
new testament criticism

Henry P. Hamann

Publishing House
St. Louis

Concordia Publishing House, St. Louis, Missouri
Copyright © 1977 Concordia Publishing House

MANUFACTURED IN THE UNITED STATES OF AMERICA

Library of Congress Cataloging in Publication Data

Hamann, Henry Paul.
    A popular guide to New Testament criticism.

    Bibliography: p.
        1. Bible.   N.T.—Criticism, interpretation, etc.
I. Title
BS2393.H34   225.6   77-9627
ISBN 0-570-03760-3

Contents

Introduction

The word "criticism" and related words like "critic," "critical," "criticize" are usually understood as referring to something negative and unpleasant. So, to the man in the street, to criticize is to find fault, and criticism is passing unfavourable judgments on the qualities of someone or something. In this book the words just mentioned are not going to be used with this negative colouring, at least not in most cases. They are going to be used more in keeping with the original meaning of the root word. A critic originally was a judge (Greek *krites*). The characteristic of a true judge is that he is fair and impartial, swaying from the truth neither to the right nor to the left. He will assess the evidence quite objectively, keeping all personal feelings and relations to the people or to the matter concerned strictly to himself, being guided in his decision purely by the facts of the case.

It is in this impartial sense that criticism should be understood in the combination "New Testament criticism." What this phrase suggests is an objective study of the books making up the New Testament (NT), a study free from all feeling, passion, and personal involvement. However, there is a big difference between what the phrase suggests and the actual situation, both past and present, that the phrase covers, and it is necessary to make a series of observations about that situation.

Much NT criticism, as a matter of fact, has been of a negative kind, with very much passing of unfavourable judgments of all kinds on NT books and writers. In part the reason for this is a reaction against the completely uncritical judgments of former days when the Bible was hardly read at all as a collection of human writings. The human side of this divine-human Scripture was given very little attention. Much criticism has been negative in the further respect that it has actually been destructive of the Christian faith; it has undermined biblical authority, weakened the case for traditional Christianity, and gnawed away at the foundations of the Christian creeds.

Now, to be quite fair, this result of biblical criticism does not in itself indicate that biblical criticism has been partial, subjective, biased. It is perfectly legitimate to argue that criticism cannot be concerned about the results of its work. It must be true to its own task, which is to find out the facts about men and things and events and literary records. And if, in

7

the process, positions once held to be true and sacred lose that esteem, well, it's too bad, but that is also the way of the world. All advance to knowledge of the truth is by way of such critical questioning and investigation.

However, it is also true that many critics of the NT have been anything but impartial and objective; rather they can be shown to have been as much determined by bias, subjective wishes, and personal commitments as men can possibly be. It must also be stated that the writer of these lines is also anything but uncommitted. The Bible is Word of God to him in a sense in which no other book or writing is Word of God. It is original, non-derivative Word of God, behind which and beyond which no one can go to arrive at something more directly Word of God, something closer to the original source of the Word, i.e., God Himself. To the writer, the Bible alone is the source of all divine truth for men, the judge of all teaching and teachers.

This conviction of the writer is no real disqualification for carrying out the task involved in the title, namely, giving an impartial account of NT criticism. All that is required for objectivity is that the reader know in advance the personal commitment of the writer he is reading. The reader can be assured of something else: that every endeavour will be made to put fairly and truthfully the positions and arguments of the critics. An objective study of NT criticism means also that the presentation must operate with premises admitted by all parties. Accordingly, this study will not operate at all with arguments based on inspiration and divine authority—not because these arguments are not part of the whole question, but because no argument or debate is possible when the basis of argument on the one side is not granted by those taking a different position. In this guide for the layman, only the premises (bases, foundations of argument) accepted by biblical critics will be recognized in the debate. Where convictions of faith have to be appealed to, it will be clear from the context that they are so, and it will be shown how different positions are often taken because of different personal convictions which cannot be given up.

The aim of this presentation of biblical criticism is to describe the whole area of criticism in a way that is intelligible to any normal, interested reader. Special attention will be given to the principles of citicism, both the principles explictly stated by critics and those not explicitly stated but presupposed. These will be critically examined, and it is hoped that, as a result of such examination, readers will be able to see what is sound and what is not, that they will be in a position to judge for themselves the value of any study, theological investigation, or commentary that comes into their hands, as they accept this and reject that with discrimination and not by mere feeling or personal choice. Readers must, in effect, learn to see themselves as judges or members of a jury with the responsibility of forming a proper judgment on the basis of the evidence provided. The scholars are the experts called to the witness stand to give their professional opinion on the evidence collected. *But they are not the judge; the reader is.* No person should ever hand over to the expert, the scholar, even if he has an international reputation, his own right and duty to judge. We can trust the average Christian to see as clearly in the important critical problems of the NT as we trust the common man to act on a jury for the determination of guilt or innocence in a complicated murder trial.

The big thing is: not to be imposed upon by mere numbers, or by the eminence, reputation, even the prodigious learning, of certain critics. The reader can be assured that scholarship and learning do not necessarily make for clear thinking. The logical incompetence of many great scholars is quite surprising, but nevertheless true. Many scholars are as much under the sway of prejudice, personal feelings, selfish ambition, even pecuniary concerns, as any common citizen. The informed reader should be in a position confidently to say that such-and-such is nonsense even if Bultmann has said it, or that So-and-So is obviously guilty of begging the question or of rationalization, even if his name is Barth. And if you don't know what the eminent scholar is saying, read somebody else. Nobody has the right to expect others to read or listen to him if he does not make the necessary effort to write or speak clearly and intelligibly. Life is too short to waste time on poor writers.

The particular aspects of criticism to be taken up in this work are: textual criticism, literary criticism, form and redaction criticism, content criticism. These four areas of criticism will make up the chapters of the book. What you can expect in their treatment are the following: a statement of the facts from which the particular problem or problems arise, in short, the occasion for the particular kind of criticism; a short history of criticism in that area; examples of critical activity; and, above all, a discussion of the principles which guide this activity.

CHAPTER ONE

Textual Criticism

It takes some effort of the imagination for people who have only seen printed newspapers and books to think themselves back to a time when all letters, documents, and lengthy books were written by hand, and all of them in one original copy. The Adelaide *Advertiser,* by way of contrast, appears daily in more than 100,000 identical copies. The books of the NT were likewise written by hand, each in one original copy.

Copies of these were, of course, made almost immediately; and for various reasons. Congregations in the vicinity of Thessalonica or Corinth, for instance, would be anxious to have in their possession a copy of the letters sent to those centres. The Letter to the Galatians was meant for a number of centres, and copying the letter would be the most expeditious way of getting it to these various places. The early Christians did a surprising amount of travelling. Aquila and Priscilla, for example, we first meet in Corinth, where they had just come from Rome as a result of the emperor's decree expelling all Jews from that city. A few years later, Paul came up with them in Ephesus, and the last chapter of the Letter to Rome suggests that when Paul wrote that letter they were back again in Rome, together with a number of other people whom Paul had first met in Asia Minor. These travellers would be anxious to take with them letters of Paul, or other apostolic writings which they had come across in their visit to some city on their travels. Papyrus was the writing-surface at that time. This is fragile like our paper, and the rolls would deteriorate quickly with use. For these and other reasons, copies of the original manuscripts were made, and copies from the copies. In course of time, the codex, something roughly resembling our book, replaced the roll, and vellum or parchment, durable writing material made from the skins of kids, lambs, and calves, took the place of papyrus. Such copying by hand continued till the time of printing, i.e., right to the middle or even the end of the 15th century.

Copying by hand means the birth of errors. Nobody will copy a lengthy piece of material without making an error or two. A poorer, less attentive, and less conscientious copier will make many mistakes. The number of errors in the manuscripts of the NT is very large. Nobody

11

knows how many errors there are, but an estimate can be made by various calculations. The known Greek manuscripts (including mere fragments) numbered 5,261 in 1969 (4,680 in 1957). Someone has counted the number of variations existing in *two* of these manuscripts: Vaticanus and 2427. These two manuscripts are closer in general than any two others in the Gospels. In St. Mark's Gospel alone, these two manuscripts differ 893 times. Take 2427 and another manuscript, Codex Bezae. These two differ in one chapter of Mark (ch. 11) 117 times. Von Soden knew about 45,000 different readings which he considered worth recording in his critical edition of the Greek NT. This was in 1913, and he and his co-workers did not work through all the manuscripts that were known then, let alone the enormous number we have now. Counting spelling mistakes (very many of these) and all kinds of obvious errors (which are hardly worth recording, since they obviously do not affect our knowledge of the text at all), we could well have more than 300,000 total variations. Even some of our best manuscripts are disfigured with errors. Codex Sinaiticus (a whole Bible, by the way, containing the Greek Old Testament as well) is said to have at least 3,000 errors due to one cause alone, that known as itacism (substituting the Greek letter "i" for other vowels). Papyrus 46, our most ancient and most important manuscript of St. Paul's letters has, according to F. C. Kenyon, 294 *singular* variants, that is, variant readings which are found only in that manuscript and nowhere else; in addition, it has 160 manifest errors.

As for the sources of variants, these are in many respects like those that take place today when any kind of copying is done by hand, whether you use a pen or a typewriter. Individual words or phrases or occasional lines are dropped; some words are repeated; spelling mistakes are made. The characteristic errors that arise from writing or typing from dictation are also found. Beside these sources of error, there are others related to the writing customs in vogue at that early date. Whole books were written in continuous script. The last sentence, for instance, if written that way would look like this: WHOLEBOOKSWEREWRITTENIN-CONTINUOUSSCRIPT. Imagine copying that sort of thing for pages without mistakes. Besides variants that arose through inadvertence for the reasons suggested, other variants were the result of deliberate changes introduced into the text for various reasons: to clear up an obscurity; to avoid doctrinal error, or to spread it; to harmonize similar sentences appearing in the first three Gospels; and for other more technical reasons as well.

This whole situation would, naturally, not need to bother us at all if we had the originals. But these have vanished long ago. The very earliest manuscript we have (Papyrus 52, containing some six verses of St. John's Gospel) is still removed by some 40 or so years from the time of the original. More complete manuscripts like Papyrus 66, with about 15 chapters of St. John's Gospel, and Papyrus 75, with some 13 chapters of Luke and a couple of John, are separated by over a century from the originals; Papyri 45 and 46 by more years still.

It may well seem that we are faced with a hopeless situation and that there is no chance of arriving at a reliable text. However, the situation is not as bad as it seems to be. For one thing, we can be sure that somewhere, in all the evidence, we have the original text. Imagine having only one or two manuscripts for the various books. Then we really would be doubtful whether we had a reliable text, for there would be so little possibility of comparison. The very quantity of evidence and variation is a check on the text and a guide to the true text. Backbreaking work indeed is involved, but the work can be done. Another consideration to be mentioned later will show that the task is not quite so difficult as it seems at this stage of the description. But one thing has become plain: the aim of textual criticism.

The Aim of Textual Criticism

The textual critic aims at nothing less than to arrive at the original form of the text he is studying. B. F. Westcott and F. J. A. Hort were so confident of the results of their work that they published a critical text of the NT in 1881—82 entitled *The New Testament in the Original Greek!* But we are running ahead of the story.

Modern scholars who have studied the Greek manuscripts of the NT, early translations of it, and quotations in church fathers have been able to point out certain facts about the whole textual tradition which considerably simplify the task of getting to the original text. They have shown that all the various witnesses to the text can be grouped in a few well-defined text-types: that characteristic of Egypt (Alexandrian or Neutral); that current in the West, in Italy, Gaul or present-day France, and North Africa (Western); and that which had its home in Constantinople, the second great centre of the Roman Empire from the early fourth century on (Byzantine or Koine). Scholars are not quite so certain about another text-type, the so-called Caesarean text. Study has also shown that the overwhelming majority of witnesses are representative of the Byzantine or Koine text. The standard text in Constantinople at the centre of the Greek Church (Rome was the centre of the Latin Church) became the standard Greek text everywhere, and was copied again and again right through the Middle Ages. The other texts, the

Alexandrian and the Caesarean, remain in comparatively few documents.

The situation really remained unchanged when printing was invented. The old texts were merely copied faster. Famous translations, like Luther's New Testament and the King James Version or Authorized Version (AV), were produced on the basis of the dominant Koine text. After 1633 this text was known as the *Textus Receptus* or Received Text (TR), and till 1831 no Greek text was printed that was not basically this TR. However, more and more scholars became doubtful whether the TR was really the text that all should receive without question. Study led to the position described at the end of the previous paragraph. The problem of the original text had become considerably clearer and more simplified by the history of the text which scholars had been able to uncover. However, the important final job of arriving at the original text still remained—and still remains. This is true in spite of the insights that had been gained. It is still necessary to determine, in every case where there is a variant reading or variant readings, which reading is the best or the right one. To this difficult but fascinating aspect of textual criticism we now turn.

The Principles of Textual Criticism

As we look at these principles we come for the first time on a distinction we meet repeatedly in biblical criticism: the difference between external and internal evidence. In textual criticism, external evidence has to do with such questions as: In what manuscripts, translations, church fathers are the readings in question to be found? How ancient are these readings, and how widely distributed are they over the Christian world (that is, the Mediterranean countries) at an early date? Westcott and Hort pinned all (or almost all) their faith on external factors in their endeavour to get back to the original text, and their influence was dominant in scholarly circles for many years. Their great principle was that, in order to restore a corrupt text (that is, a text which appears only in copies marred by errors), one must uncover its history. This means trying to establish the genealogy of a text, by working back to the original from a proper study of all its descendants.

Suppose this situation. A teacher dictates a lengthy piece of written material to a group of three students. The teacher we shall designate A, and the pupils B(1), B(2), and B(3). Now, there will be errors in each of the pupils' versions. These versions will each show a different pattern of errors. Now, suppose further that each of the three students has his version copied by 10 other people. There will now be 10 different copies of B(1), each of which will have new errors, besides keeping the errors of B(1). The same will be true of B(2) and B(3). The new copies we shall call C(1), 10 copies; C(2), 10 copies; C(3), 10 copies. Now, imagine that A is lost irretrievably, and so also B(1), B(2), and B(3). We have only the 30 C copies. Study of these will divide them up into three groups, corresponding to the three students. Further study will lead infallibly to the actual form of B(1), B(2), and B(3), as each group of 10 is studied to find out what was common and original to it. Similarly, from B(1), B(2), and B(3), now recovered, we shall be able to recover A by the same careful comparison of their material. We shall be able to do this infallibly, with an absolutely certain result.

The application of this principle to the Greek NT, however, proved to be a failure. And the reasons for this are two. First, there are too many gaps in the transmission. There is no complete genealogy as I supposed in my A, B, C example. And, secondly, there is too much mixture in the genealogy. Copies were made not only from one, but from more manuscripts; the lines of descent were not kept separate but were often crossed with others. So external evidence by itself cannot reach the goal we want: the restoration of the original text of the NT. However, external evidence does indicate the limits within which the textual critic must work. He will not consider a reading unless it goes back to an early period, say to the second century. Nor will he normally pay much attention to a reading which has no great geographical spread when it is opposed by one with widespread attestation in independent witnesses. But it still remains true that external evidence cannot determine the right reading in any disputed passage. Internal or intrinsic evidence must come to its aid, and the two together will in most cases lead to a pretty definite conclusion. It can be said that a good 90 to 95 per cent of the NT text is quite certain. In the case of the disputed readings very little real difference of meaning takes place in many instances, no matter which reading offered by the witnesses is chosen. No part of the faith is affected in any of these disputed passages.

The goal of *internal* evidence is to find what is called the *original* reading, that is, we look for the reading which explains all the variants but which is not in turn explained by them. This sounds good, and in principle it is good. The trouble is that in many cases it is as possible to argue the one way as it is the other, and to make out a good case for the original reading by arguing for or against a particular variant.

Another principle, subsidiary to the one just mentioned, runs: The more difficult reading is the original meaning. This dictum, however, is not by any means always true. Every mistake accidentally introduced into a sentence will tend to make the sentence more difficult. Take the sentence: "In the beginning was the Word." Suppose that through an accidental omission of a word we found in a manuscript: "In the beginning was the . . ." The omission of that one word would destroy the meaning of the sentence, and it would be impossible to guess at the lost word with anything approaching certainty. The principle of the correctness of the difficult reading seems very doubtful to me, and it is probably more often inapplicable than suitable.

"The reading which is not a harmonizing reading is likely to be correct." This assertion has a special applicability in the first three Gospels. In these we frequently find the same story or incident described, or the same sentence of Jesus quoted, in much the same language. The tendency for copyists was to write a sentence of Jesus in the familiar form, to write a sentence in Matthew just as it is in Mark, or a well-known sentence in Luke as it was remembered from Matthew, no matter how the words actually run in the manuscript from which the copying is being done. For example, the third petition of the Lord's Prayer is omitted in many manuscripts of Luke, and most modern translations do not print it as part of Luke's text. However, in the tradition there are manuscripts which do have the third petition. Most scholars would say that the reading which endeavours to bring about a harmonization between the texts of Matthew and Luke in the Lord's Prayer is deliberate, that the harmonizing reading is therefore not original, and that the original wording of the Lord's Prayer in Luke did not have the third petition.

"The more crude, less-polished reading is the right reading." This dictum, too, cannot be applied without caution. We have to know what sort of copier we are dealing with, whether he was a master of language or not. Not all copyists were learned men and masters of language. It is just as easy to imagine a clumsy copyist making material he is copying cruder, as it is to imagine a learned corrector making it more graceful. So the principle would be right sometimes, but wrong at other times.

Try another dictum: "The proper reading is one which accords with the style of the writer." Here again, we have to say Yes and No. On the face of it, the dictum seems sound enough. If we have an expression which cannot be duplicated in a person's writings and which is different from the expressions we do find there for expressing a certain idea, then we could have a pointer to the right reading in a particular case. But when do we (that is, the experts in language) *know* a person's style? When we have a great deal of a person's writing to go by, we can say we know his style, and we can with some assurance say that he could not have written such-and-such. I have my doubts whether we know enough about any writer of the NT to be able to say that. We have enough material about Paul to be able to say: "This is characteristic of Paul," but it is doubtful whether we have enough from his pen to be able to say: "Paul could not have written such-and-such." You have to know a lot more about a writer to be able to make the negative judgment!

I have left for the last principle the one which is encountered most often: "The shorter reading is likely to be the right one." I do this, because I hold that this is so often wrong as to be valueless. The experience of all people who work as editors and who must spend much time proofreading, correcting the copy being got ready for printers, is that omission of words, phrases, and occasionally whole lines and even paragraphs, is a common occurrence. Rarely does a copyist add material, except the very common thing of duplicating a word or succession of words ("and and"). A copyist may occasionally fall into an equivalent phrase ("began" instead of "start," for instance—that sort of thing), but other additions to and expansions of a text being copied rarely happen. The only case that can be imagined as happening in ancient times with the NT material is that a copyist mistakenly took into the text some note that a reader put into the margin or between the lines. Otherwise, simple copying regularly results in omissions from a text, not additions to it.

In the art of textual criticism it is important not to be guided by *one* principle alone. This is the surest way to making a mistake. Textual criticism requires the judicious application of all the principles of criticism, both those relating to external evidence and those having to do with internal evidence.

A few examples of what textual criticism does, and can do, will probably help the reader as much as a detailed discussion of theoretical principles.

Take a very famous sentence of Jesus: "Father, forgive them; for they know not what they do" (Luke 23:34). This sentence is found in only one of the important early Greek manuscripts (Sinaiticus), but a correction there suggests that omission is the proper reading. Important manuscripts representing Alexandrian, Western, and Caesarean text-types omit it. The older manuscript of the Old Syriac, the Egyptian translations, and some manuscripts of the Old Latin also give a negative vote. The omission, then, has early and widespread attestation. The Koine has the sentence, but since this is a late form of the text, little weight can be given to the many manuscripts of this text-type. When we turn to arguments based on internal evidence, it is hard to find any good reason why the sentence should be omitted if it were there originally. It is so clearly in keeping with the whole mind of Christ and the whole Christian Gospel that a deliberate omission seems just beyond the realm of possibility. An accidental omission is more likely, but only just. Lengthy accidental omissions are rare, in any case. I think we can rule out accidental omission or accidental addition of this sentence. On the other hand, it is rather easy to imagine the deliberate addition of this sentence, if it were not there originally. And once it was added, it would of course be copied again and again. We have a case where, to this writer at least, the establishing of the original reading seems comparatively easy. The omission of the sentence, if it were there originally, is not to be explained, but its addition, if it were not there originally, is explained without difficulty. So the argument from internal evidence joins hands with the argument from external evidence, and casts strong doubt on this very famous saying being part of the original text of Luke. This is, to be sure, far different from saying that it is something Jesus never said. If any sentence looks like an original sentence of Jesus, this is it. The echo of Jesus' words in Stephen's statement: "Lord, do not hold this sin against them" (Acts 7:60) strongly supports this judgment. So we must imagine that somebody, missing this sentence of Jesus in the copy of Luke's Gospel in his possession, added it, thus preserving this sentence of Jesus, to the eternal gratitude of the church.

In Rev. 1:5 we have an interesting example of the change in translation that can be involved because of one Greek letter. The AV has: "Unto him that loved us, and *washed* (the Greek word: *lousanti*) us from our sins in his own blood . . ." The Revised Standard Version (RSV) has: "To him who loves us and has *freed* (the Greek word: *lusanti*) us from our sins by his blood . . ." The external evidence slightly favours the word translated "freed," and most modern translations have adopted this reading, but not all. But the weight of evidence the one way is not so strong as to be decisive. The argument on internal grounds is very even. The letter "o" could very easily have been dropped in transcription. On the other hand, here is a case where an attentive and intelligent scribe could easily have added the letter mentioned, arguing that "washed" fitted the sentence even better than "freed" because of the reference to the blood of Jesus. One critical text suggests that there may be reminiscences of the Old Testament (OT) here: "And he will redeem (that is, free) Israel from all his iniquities" (Ps. 130:8) and "that her iniquity is pardoned" (Isa. 40:2, where the ancient Greek translation called the Septuagint has "freed"). But neither place is really close to the Revelation passage, and neither has any reference to blood. Here is a case where we find ourselves like a donkey between two bales of straw, not knowing which one to go for. Also, the actual difference in meaning involved in the two words is very slight.

The lack of important difference in the final instance as a result of a different reading may be illustrated by another case, where the actual reading is next door to certain. Many of us know the Gloria in Excelsis best in the words of the AV: "Glory to God in the highest, and on earth peace, good will toward men" (Luke 2:14). The RSV, reflected in the liturgy of the Australian *Lutheran Hymnal*, has:

Glory to God in the highest,
and on earth peace among men with whom he is pleased.

If we wrote the AV translation similarly as poetry we would get:

Glory to God in the highest,
and on earth peace,
good will toward men.

The difference in translation arises from the presence or absence of one Greek letter: the AV translators used a text with the Greek word *eudokia* (goodwill), while the RSV accepted the text with the Greek word *eudokias* (of goodwill). Here the Caesarean and late Koine texts are, speaking generally, opposed by the Alexandrian and Western text-types. This is in itself pretty decisive for the RSV translation. But the Qumran literature has made this reading, as I said, next door to certain, for there we find a phrase "children of His good will," which is the equivalent of the two Greek words translated by "men with whom he is pleased." Internal evidence is again quite indecisve. Transcriptional possibilities and probabilities work both ways; the poetry of the lines is just as good with the three-line AV grouping as with the two-line RSV rendering, perhaps even a little more choice. But what difference arises for the total meaning? None that I can see. The "good will" in both cases must refer to that of God toward men. The common way in which part of the Gloria is used at Christmas, "men of good will," that is, men who have goodwill and are characterized by it as opposed to others who are not— this is not the meaning of the Gloria, whether you take the one or the other reading, whether you go by the AV or by the RSV.

19

CHAPTER TWO
Literary Criticism

"Literary criticism" in this chapter and in the whole book is to be used in a very restricted sense. It will concern merely the correctness of traditional views concerning the NT writings, whether these are put forward by the writings themselves or whether they go back to early church tradition. The measure of judgment will be the character of the writings themselves. Questions like the following are involved: Is the particular writing integral, i.e., one complete writing, or composite, the result of a number of separate contributions? Is the writer the person said to be the writer in the book or the person traditionally associated with that book? Or is the work actually assigned wrongly to the traditional author? Or is it impossible to determine who the author is?

Literary criticism often, perhaps even usually, takes in many other questions besides those mentioned. It could concern itself with the actual language of the writing, the aesthetic character of the writing, its roots in other literature, or its effects on other literature. It could include form criticism and redaction criticism. It could take up the relation of form and content. It could institute a comparison between NT writings and their form as a whole with that of contemporary and near-contemporary writings of Greece and Rome. There are other areas of study, besides, which could be included in the literary-critical study of the NT writings. I have fixed on the particular aspect of literary criticism described above because it is actually an important part of literary criticism. Besides, it is easy to describe, to talk about, to understand. It also illustrates the critical method particularly well.

Literary criticism, like textual criticism, is a development of modern times, having its real beginnings in the 18th century. Forerunners were men like Spinoza, Jean Astruc, Richard Simon. Occasional critical statements of a literary nature are found even earlier. There is the famous discussion of the relation between the Revelation of St. John and the Gospel of St. John by Dionysius of Alexandria. Dionysius (d. 264) is quoted in Eusebius' *Ecclesiastical History* to the following effect:

> After completing the whole, one might say, of his prophecy, the prophet calls those blessed who observe it and indeed himself also; for he says:

"Blessed is he that keepeth the words of the prophecy of this book, and I John, he that saw and heard these things." That, then, he was certainly named John and that this book is by one John, I will not gainsay; for I fully allow that it is the work of some holy and inspired person. But I should not readily agree that he was the apostle, the son of Zebedee, the brother of James, whose are the Gospel entitled According to John and the Catholic Epistle. For I form my judgment from the character of each and from the nature of the language and from what is known as the general construction of the book, that the John therein mentioned is not the same. For the evangelist nowhere adds his name, nor yet proclaims himself, throughout either the Gospel or the Epistle.

This is really modern in every way, and what Dionysius does, comparing two writings in big matters and in small, is just the method of your modern critic also.

There is another famous piece of literary criticism, and that is Luther's rejection of the Epistle of James. Luther compares the way Paul speaks about justification (for example, in Romans 4 and Galatians 2 and 3) with the statements of James in ch. 2. He points out that James uses Gen. 15:6 and the reference to Abraham quite differently, or even in an opposite way, from Paul. And his conclusion is that the Letter of James cannot be the writing of an apostle because of this contradiction and for other reasons as well. Similar criticism on his part led him to regard Hebrews, Revelation, and the Letter of Jude as nonapostolic writings.

In spite of these interesting and important examples of literary criticism in earlier centuries of the church—there are other examples as well—the statement is still true that literary criticism of the NT is a development of modern times.

It will be convenient to show literary criticism at work in the NT by the use of some few examples. These are the following: certain epistles of St. Paul, especially Ephesians and the Pastoral Letters (1 and 2 Timothy and Titus), 2 Peter, and the Synoptic Gospels (Matthew, Mark, and Luke). In each case the traditional position will be contrasted with the critical one, and the critical position will be examined and assessed. However, a few preliminary observations of a more general nature concerning types of evidence will be necessary.

As with textual criticism, so with literary criticism one must distinguish between external and internal evidence. External evidence includes such things as the following: the claim of the writing in question; the testimony to it in the early centuries following; quotations of its material by other writers, either directly or indirectly confirming or accepting the claim of the writing in question; and, of course, quotations which imply non-acceptance of the writing's claims. In the case of anonymous writings, external evidence means the tradition concerning a writing, and its acceptance or rejection in the early centuries following its appearance. Internal evidence has to do with aspects of a writing which are (or seem to be) in conflict with its claims concerning itself. These aspects include such matters as the writer's language and style, his theological assertions, and historical hints and implications.

These two classes of evidence are by no means on the same level. External evidence is by so much the stronger that one needs an absolutely unassailable argument on internal grounds to overthrow it. This is all the more the situation when we are dealing with literary works that were written so many centuries before our time and in societies (the Christian congregations) of which we know so very little when all is said and done. I may be able to demonstrate that a student of mine is not really the writer of an article he has handed in but that he has cribbed the whole from a book in the library. I know the writer, his abilities, his normal style and method of getting at things, and also the possible sources of the material in the library. I am in a favourable position to allow internal evidence to win the victory over the false claim. I can confront him with the evidence and will in most cases have no difficulty in extracting a confession. However, if a student has been very clever in his use of other material, I may miss the plagiarism altogether, or may never be able to demonstrate that such illegal borrowing has taken place, if the student insists that he has done no such thing. Even in the favourable circumstances just mentioned, it is very difficult indeed to win with an argument based wholly on internal evidence. It is obvious that the situation becomes far more difficult still with the letters of St. Paul and other NT writings. Internal evidence in such a case must be comparatively impotent. Only a clear anachronism will be powerful enough to overthrow the force of the argument from external evidence.

A good example of the last point, overthrowing a claim through the uncovering of an anachronism, is that supplied by the so-called Donation of Constantine. This is the name given to a supposed grant by the emperor Constantine the Great to Pope Silvester I (314—335) and to his successors of spiritual supremacy in the whole church and of temporal dominion over Rome, Italy, and the entire Western world. As is now generally recognized, this was a fabrication dating from the end of the eighth century. The genuineness of the document was first questioned in 1440 by Lorenzo Valla, but its genuineness was defended till about the end of the 18th century. The document operates with a feudal concept of society which did not arise in Europe till centuries after Constantine. This anachronism demonstrates to the hilt that the claim of the document is a false one. However, it should be borne in mind as well that the external evidence in this case is also very poor, no references to it appearing until five centuries after it is said to have been written.

To turn now to our examples. The Letter to the Ephesians is frequently declared by modern scholars to be non-Pauline. The only matter which might be considered at all to be a gap in the external evidence for the letter as one by the apostle is that some manuscripts omit the words "at Ephesus" in the first verse. Of course, this does not really cast any doubt on the author; it only raises some doubt as to the people to whom the author wrote. The attacks on Pauline authorship are chiefly concerned with style and language. English readers are not likely to be struck by such matters, for translations in any case tend to reflect the style of the translator(s) rather than the style of the orignal author. However, even they may sense, for instance, that the opening section sounds somewhat wordy and laboured, with an unusual fullness of expression, and the thought moves only slowly. The letter's closeness to Colossians (about three-fifths of which is reflected in Ephesians), joined with curious differences of meaning in similar phrases, causes doubts in scholars. Almost all Pauline letters seem to have echoes in Ephesians, a fact which arouses the suspicion that Ephesians is a late production. Further doubts arise from different doctrinal emphases, most of these striking the present writer as quite minute. It seems impossible to me to demonstrate from these points of criticism that Paul could not have written the letter. A modern scholar (Robert Grant) asks the question: "Which is more likely—that we can determine the authenticity of a letter written ninety or ninety-five percent in accordance with Paul's style, and his outlook, or that we cannot?" His answer: "We are not in a position to judge, and since the authenticity of the letter cannot be disproved it should be regarded as genuine." The very fact that eminent scholars are found on both sides of the argument shows that the case against Pauline authorship is very weak. On evidence like this you could never condemn a man in a court of law; he would not even be brought to trial.

A stronger case can be made out for the critical view of the Pastoral Epistles. Again, the external evidence is *for* their Pauline authorship. They were transmitted together with the other Pauline letters, except in one instance to be mentioned in a moment. We are informed by Tertullian that the Gnostics Basilides (about A.D. 130) and Marcion (about 140) rejected them, although his statement may mean no more than that these Gnostics did not know them. Besides, Marcion was quite dogmatic about what he accepted as NT writings and what he did not, and the contents of the Pastorals quite definitely would not be his cup of tea. So here in Marcion we have uncertainty at the best, or special pleading at the worst. A very important early codex (Chester Beatty papyrus 46) of Paul's letters does not contain the Pastorals. But the codex is defective, some 14 pages, seven at the front and seven at the end, having been lost. The missing letters (2 Thessalonians and Philemon are also missing) could not have been written on the missing pages. But the copyist may have made a miscalculation as to the number of pages required for his codex. Of course, he could have stuck extra pages on at the end, but they would in that case have been lost with the 14 mentioned. So where are we? We are left with the absence of material, and from this non-existent evidence we can make no conclusions at all. The Pastorals may not have been in the original codex, but they also may have been there.

On internal grounds there is some room for doubting Pauline authorship. The writer does not write at all like the Paul we know in the generally-accepted letters, and this difference probably shows up in translations as well.

Besides this difficulty, there is the historical situation, which presupposes a series of events and situations different from what we know of Paul's life from his other letters and the Acts of the Apostles. The incidental comments in the Pastorals almost necessarily lead to the view that Paul was set free after the imprisonment in Rome referred to at the end of Acts, and that he was active in Crete, Greece, and Asia Minor before being recaptured and brought to Rome for a further imprisonment, trial, and death. Second Timothy suggests that Paul knows the end to be near. However, nothing in all this is really impossible from a historical point of view, or even improbable. Difficulties are caused by further facts like the following: that Paul intended to go to Spain after getting to Rome (Rom. 15:23-29), and that he actually did so according to 1 Clement 5:7; that he regarded his work in the East as ended (Rom. 15:23), and that he did not expect to see the elders of Ephesus again (Acts 20:25). But there is no insuperable difficulty even with these added considerations. The future is not predictable even by St. Paul. Man proposes, but God disposes, as we have often heard. What Paul had in mind and intended in the year 58 may not have been possible or even desirable four or five years later. Even if the Pastorals were non-genuine, they would be strong evidence for renewed journeys of Paul in the East and a second imprisonment. Inventions like this would be hard to get credence for if they were actually untrue. Besides, the facts stand in some tension with the tradition of activity in the West. So there is no reason to attack the genuineness of the Pastorals because of the new situations contained in them. The Pastorals are rather a source of historical value for Paul's last years.

The attack on the Pastorals because of historical considerations includes also the claim that the Pastorals reflect a situation in the life of the church which is later than that found in his other writings. That a difference exists between the picture of church life unfolded by the recognized Pauline letters and that of the Pastorals, every reader of the two will see. But both pictures could be true of the time of Paul, particularly if we bear in mind differences of place and time. Even the church organization in the Pastorals is a very simple one, and it is not hard to imagine such a simple organization arising almost at once when organization of some sort was felt to be necessary. Also, different congregations could well have developed differently. The point is that we just do not know enough of the actual life and history of the apostolic age to say what could not have happened. And where we do not know, it is the proper thing to say nothing.

We have mentioned language difficulties, historical difficulties. To these must be added a different theological outlook. Here again we are dealing with something that every student will observe for himself. But it is one thing to say that there are differences of theological emphasis and outlook; it is quite another to say that Paul could not have written Romans and the Pastorals, or that the Pastorals are wrongly and falsely ascribed to him.

The last sentence above suggests a solution of the problem of the Pastorals frequently found among defenders of their authenticity: that Paul made use of a secretary to whom he gave a considerable amount of freedom in formulating what he wanted to say to Timothy and Titus. The use of secretaries by busy men is well attested in Roman times. In a number of letters Paul associates other writers with himself as co-authors of the letters (for example, 1 and 2 Thessalonians, 2 Corinthians, Philippians, Colossians). Peter says in so many words that he used Silvanus as such a secretary (1 Peter 5:12), although this reading of the verse is disputed by some. Since the Pastorals are so much of a piece in style and theological outlook, Paul must have been served by the same secretary for them all. The hypothesis of a secretary would explain to the full all the difficulties set for the genuineness of the letters by their language, style, and theological flavour.

If the opposers of the genuineness of the Pauline letters so far referred to were correct in their judgment, then we would have in the NT a considerable body of pseudonymous writings. Some comments on pseudonymity seem to be called for.

We are well acquainted with the custom of using a pseudonym (a false name) in literature. Pseudonyms have been used for protection by the authors of heretical or subversive literature when the publishing of that sort of material could result in imprisonment or worse. When it was not considered respectable for women to be writers, women authors resorted to the pseudonym. So we have the famous writer George Eliot, a pseudonym for Mary Anne Evans. Mark Twain, the writer of *The Adventures of Tom Sawyer* and *The Adventures of Huckleberry Finn*, was actually Samuel Clemens. And there are many other famous pseudonyms besides, including Voltaire (Francois Marie Arouet), who is claimed to have used at least 137 pseudonyms. There is in this practice no wicked intent to deceive, although deception of a kind is, of course, involved. But the case is different if a writer passes off his writings under the name of an actual person, and a famous person at that. This is what is involved in the claim that such and such letters of the NT are pseudonymous. It is often claimed that the ancients saw no harm in this sort of thing, that the writer who used such a pseudonym might even be acting from good motives, to honour the man chosen as the ostensible writer, or humbly to keep his own person in the background. Whether this claim is true may well be doubted. We actually have an example of an early Christian who acted in the way suggested, but who was punished for his action. In a writing of the church father Tertullian we find the story.

> If those who read the writings that falsely bear the name of Paul adduce the examples of Thecla to maintain the right of women to teach and baptize, let them know that the presbyter in Asia who produced this document, as if he could by himself add anything to the prestige of Paul, was removed from his office after he had been convicted and had confessed that he did it out of love for Paul.

What we know of pseudonymous writings in the early church does not at all help the case of those who claim that so many letters of the NT are pseudonymous. There is a very large array of works (apocryphal we call them) to which the names of apostolic men are attached. These works follow, in the main, the divisions of the NT which we know so well: Gospels, Acts, Epistles, Apocalypses. So we have all sorts of apocryphal Gospels ascribed to apostolic men. Also apocryphal Acts are found in numbers, and the same is the case with Apocalypses. And these are generally known by apostolic names. But the numbers of pseudapostolic letters (letters falsely ascribed to apostles) is comparatively small. The letter form did not in fact belong to the popular types of apocryphal literature. We can guess why. You do not need the same imagination to concoct a "Gospel" or an "Acts" as you do to write an imaginary letter. The letter is far more personal in form, not narrative at all, and even the unwary will shy at the difficulty. It is all the more surprising, then, given this comparative infrequence of pseudapostolic letters, to find present-day scholars pointing out so many among the 21 letters of the NT; more than half are more or less confidently claimed to be wrongly (falsely) ascribed to the men whom the letters claim to be the authors.

A comparison of generally-acknowledged pseudonymous letters and those claimed to be such in the NT is support for the traditional view. It is well known that the many apocryphal Gospels cut a very poor figure in comparison with the authentic Gospels. They are excluded as possible claimants for a place in the NT by the abject spiritual poverty of their contents. The same is the case with the pseudapostolic letters. They proclaim themselves to be non-apostolic by their contents. Those men, whoever they were, who took to producing writings to match those of the NT, claiming apostolic men as their writers, were men whose capabilities were on a par with the low character of their intentions. The letters whose genuineness is doubted are not on that level at all. Some of them, particularly Ephesians and 1 Peter, are on the level of the most excellent NT writings. Forgers just do not turn out work like this. To use the words of our Lord with a new twist, "You will know them by their fruits. . . .So, every sound tree bears good fruit, but the bad tree bears evil fruit" (Matt. 7:16-17).

In only one writing of the NT can a good case be made out for its being pseudonymous, and that is Second Peter. In the case of this writing there is a convergence of arguments from external evidence and internal evidence, all pointing strongly in one direction. The letter strongly claims to have been written by the apostle Peter: 1:1, 14, 16; 3:1. The very insistence on the person of Peter in these passages is the sort of thing a forger would do. But the letter is not mentioned or referred to till the beginning of the third century. Origen, the first real witness, about the middle of the third century, speaks of it with hesitation. This late knowledge of the letter fits in with the fact that a number of writings ascribed to Peter, but pseudonymously, appeared about the middle of the second century. To these facts of external evidence must be added those supplied by internal evidence. There is the relation of 2 Peter to the short Letter of Jude. Jude and 2 Peter 2 are so close together that one of the writers must have used the other, and the likelihood seems all the one way, that Jude was first. But this in turn puts 2 Peter late, later than the death of Peter. Again, a comparison of 1 Peter and 2 Peter makes it extremely unlikely that the same writer produced both letters. There are, besides, certain expressions in 2 Peter which point to a date later than the '60s of the first century. These are found in 3:2, the conjunction of prophets, the Lord, and the apostles; in 3:4, which looks back to the end of the first generation of the church; and in 3:16, which presupposes a collection of Paul's letters, which in turn are on a level with the OT Scriptures. Defenders of the traditional view try to weaken the force of these arguments and advance others in defence of the Petrine authorship, but to the present writer this seems a pretty desperate defence.

It will be helpful to take some examples of literary criticism at work in the question of the *integrity* of NT writings. We think of 2 Corinthians as one complete letter, with its address at the beginning, its various matters discussed in the body of the letter, and the concluding greeting and benediction. However, very many scholars see at least four different letters combined in one: (a) chapters 1—7; (b) chapters 8 and 9; (c) chapters 10—13; and (d) the little section 6:14—7:1. (One scholar, Willi Marxsen, finds no fewer than six such snippets.) It is not the authorship of the four sections which is doubted—scholars are pretty well agreed that they are all written by Paul—but their fittingness in the one letter. It seems to the critics to be psychologically impossible for such heterogeneous material to be found in one letter. Everybody finds difficulty with the little section 6:14—7:1, which seems to be out of place not only where it is now found, but even in the letter as a whole. However, opinions differ with the other sections, and there are many who will hold to the integrity of the letter as it stands. I think one only needs to think of one's own letters to remember that lengthy letters are not necessarily completed on the one day, and to recall how we digress and then return to a subject previously taken up, just as the mood and spirit dictate. Letters are rarely planned to fit ideals of composition. It seems an unnecessary piece of criticism to find a number of letters or pieces of letters combined in 2 Corinthians, in defiance of the whole manuscript tradition, including that of the translations; in all of these 2 Corinthians appears as an integral whole. Given the character of letters generally, there seems to be no sensible reason for urging internal evidence against external evidence. The very same considerations may be urged against those who suspect the integrity of Philippians. It has something of a miscellaneous character about it as it is, so to lop off part of it as not in keeping with the rest (namely, 3:2-21) is quite pedantic. Some even more powerful adjective is needed to describe the view of those who see some three letters fused together in Philippians.

However, something of a case can be made for the view that the 16th chapter of Romans was not really intended for the congregation at that place. It is not that the internal evidence is stronger here than in the cases mentioned earlier, but here we have manuscript evidence which suggests that there is something strange about ch. 16 and that the letter might have finished at 15:33. Verse 20 of ch. 16 looks like another ending, and so does 16:24. The internal evidence, by the way, is as follows: the list of greetings suggests an extraordinary number of acquaintances of the apostle in Rome; some of these are closely associated with the province of Asia (chief city: Ephesus); the sharp warning against Judaizers in Rom. 16:17-20 does not fit the cautious way in which Paul addresses and deals with a congregation not known to him and which he wants to win over to the support of his missionary plans.

The really big example of literary criticism in the NT is the so-called "Synoptic problem." A great deal of energy has been expended on this problem over many years, well over a century, but it cannot really be said that it has been solved, although a number of scholars speak with a great deal of assurance about the finality of the commonly-held solution. But, first, we must briefly describe the problem.

The first three Gospels are marked by many striking similarities. There is the same basic course of events: the ministry in Galilee, the movement to Jerusalem, death and resurrection in that city; and in all of them the account of the end in Jerusalem is by far the most comprehensive of all accounts of Jesus' doings. Many incidents are told in very similar language. The similarity of the Synoptic Gospels stands out all the more clearly when they are compared with the Fourth Gospel, the character of which is quite different. It is this basic similarity of viewpoint which gives us the term "synoptic," meaning "looked at from the same point of view."

On the other hand, there are many points in which the individual Synoptics differ from their fellows, and the combination of the great similarities and strange differences makes up the Synoptic problem. It is doubtful whether the real complexity of the problem was seen for many centuries, although no observant and careful reader could have been quite oblivious of it. According to the church tradition, the Synoptics were written in the order in which they appear in our Bibles: Matthew, Mark, Luke. It is church tradition also which tells us the writers' names, for all the Gospels are anonymous, unlike the NT letters. There is a further tradition which asserts that Matthew's Gospel was originally written in Hebrew (i.e., Aramaic).

Some more detailed observations are in place. When we look at the order of the incidents which are common to all three Synoptics, we find there is here also a remarkable consistency. Apart from the material in Matthew 8 and 9, and a few other incidents (like the calling and sending of the Twelve, ch. 10), the order of material is the same in Matthew and Mark. Divergences from a common order are still less consequential in Luke's Gospel. Almost all of Mark is found both in Matthew and in Luke. But Matthew and Luke have a considerable body of material which is not found in Mark. Much of this material common to Matthew and Luke is found in a corresponding order, but there is also a great deal which is apart from this order. Both Matthew and Luke have much material besides, which is peculiar to each of them respectively. Marcan peculiarities, on the other hand, consist of only a few verses.

A further, most important aspect of the similarities (and differences) between the Synoptic Gospels is contained in the language which is found in the parallel paragraphs and sentences. A knowledge of the original Greek in which the Gospels are written is necessary to make a completely satisfactory study of this side of the problem. However, some idea can be obtained of the situation also from translations. A number of parallel sections is here supplied. A careful, line-by-line, verse-by-verse, comparison will give the reader some idea of the similarity of language, as well as of differences within the similarity. The translation used is that of the RSV, and the material is taken by permission from Reuben J. Swanson, *The Horizontal Line Synopsis of the Gospels* (Dillsboro: Western North Carolina Press, Inc., 1975). The reader should note that the lead text is wholly underlined, as well as all correspondence with it in the other Gospels. The first three examples are to illustrate the material common to Matthew, Mark, and Luke; the other two are examples of material common to Matthew and Luke, what is known as "Q" material.

Example 1. The Appearance of John

```
Mk 1.2    As it                          is written in
M  3.3a   For this is he      who        was spoken of                          by
L  3.4a   As it                          is written in the book of the words of
```

```
Mk  1.2   Isaiah the prophet,
M   3.3   the prophet Isaiah when he said,
L   3.4   Isaiah the prophet,


Mk  1.2              "Behold, I send my messenger before thy face,


Mk  1.2              who shall prepare thy way;


Mk  1.3              the voice of one crying in the wilderness:
M   3.3             "The voice of one crying in the wilderness:
L   3.4             "The voice of one crying in the wilderness:


Mk  1.3              Prepare      the way of the Lord,
M   3.3              Prepare      the way of the Lord,
L   3.4              Prepare      the way of the Lord,


Mk  1.3              make his paths straight--"
M   3.3              make his paths straight."
L   3.4              make his paths straight.


Mk  1.4                                                  John the baptizer
M   3.1                              came                 John the Baptist,
L   3.2   Caiaphas, the word of God came            to   John the son of

Mk  1.4   appeared  in the wilderness,
M   3.1   preaching in the wilderness                          of
L   3.3   Zechariah in the wilderness; and he went into all the region about the


Mk  1.4             preaching a baptism of repentance for the forgiveness of sins.
M   3.2   Judea,                     "Repent,    for the kingdom of heaven is
L   3.3   Jordan, preaching a baptism of repentance for the forgiveness of sins.


Mk  1.5   And there went out to him          all the country of Judea, and all
M   3.5   Then        went out to him Jerusalem and all              Judea  and all


Mk  1.5   the people of      Jerusalem;  and they were baptized by him in the river
M   3.6   the region about the Jordan,   and they were baptized by him in the river


Mk  1.6   Jordan, confessing their sins.  Now John was  clothed with camel's hair,
M   3.4   Jordan, confessing their sins.  Now John wore a garment of camel's hair,


Mk  1.6   and had a leather girdle around his waist, and     ate      locusts and
M   3.4   and       a leather girdle around his waist; and his food was locusts and


Mk  1.7   wild honey.
M   3.4   wild honey.
```

Example 2. The Healing of a Paralytic

```
Mk  2.1    And                                          when he    returned
M   9.1    And getting into a boat                      he         crossed over and


Mk  2.1         to     Capernaum after some   days, it was reported that he was at
M   9.1    came to his own city.
L   5.17                    On one of those days, as he was teaching,


Mk  2.2    home.  And many were                              gathered together,
L   5.17              there were Pharisees and teachers of the law sitting by, who


Mk  2.2    so that there was no longer room for them, not even about the door; and
L   5.17    had come from every village of Galilee and Judea and from Jerusalem; and


Mk  2.3    he was preaching the word to them.        And          they came,
M   9.2                                              And behold,  they
L   5.18   the power of the Lord was with him to heal. And behold, men  were


Mk  2.3    bringing to him    a          paralytic  carried by four men.
M   9.2    brought   to him   a          paralytic, lying on his bed;
L   5.18   bringing on a bed a man who was paralyzed, and they sought to bring him


Mk  2.4                               And when they could not get near him because
L   5.19   in and lay him before Jesus; but finding no way to bring him in,  because


Mk  2.4    of the crowd, they removed    the roof above him; and when they had made
L   5.19   of the crowd, they went up on the roof           and


Mk  2.4    an opening, they let    down      the pallet on which the paralytic lay.
L   5.19                     let him down with his bed through the tiles into the midst


Mk  2.5                    And when Jesus saw their faith,
M   9.2                    and when Jesus saw their faith
L   5.20   before Jesus.  And when he     saw their faith


Mk  2.5             he said to the paralytic,          "My son, your sins are
M   9.2             he said to the paralytic, "Take heart, my son; your sins are
L   5.20            he said,                            "Man, your sins are


Mk  2.6    forgiven."      Now       some of the scribes were sitting there,
M   9.3    forgiven."      And behold, some of the scribes
L   5.21   forgiven you."  And                the scribes and the Pharisees began to


Mk  2.7    questioning    in their hearts, "Why does this man speak thus? It is
M   9.3              said to themselves,        "This man              is
L   5.21   question, saying,               "Who is this that speaks


Mk  2.8    blasphemy!   Who can forgive sins but God alone?" And immediately
M   9.4    blaspheming."                                     But
L   5.22   blasphemies? Who can forgive sins but God only?"  When
```

32

```
Mk  2.8   Jesus, perceiving in his spirit that they thus questioned within themselves,
M   9.4   Jesus, knowing                     their     thoughts,
L   5.22  Jesus  perceived                   their     questionings,              he


Mk  2.9   said  to them, "Why do you question thus in your hearts?      Which is
M   9.5   said,          "Why do you think evil     in your hearts? For which is
L   5.23  answered them, "Why do you question       in your hearts?      Which is


Mk  2.9   easier, to say to the paralytic, 'Your sins are forgiven,'    or to say,
M   9.5   easier, to say,                  'Your sins are forgiven,'    or to say,
L   5.23  easier, to say,                  'Your sins are forgiven you,' or to say,


Mk  2.10  'Rise, take up your pallet and walk'? But that you may know that the Son
M   9.6   'Rise                      and walk'? But that you may know that the Son
L   5.24  'Rise                      and walk'? But that you may know that the Son


Mk  2.10  of man has authority on earth to forgive sins"--he      said to the
M   9.6   of man has authority on earth to forgive sins"--he then said to the
L   5.24  of man has authority on earth to forgive sins"--he      said to the man


Mk  2.11          paralytic-- "I say to you, rise, take up your pallet  and go
M   9.6          paralytic--               "Rise, take up your bed     and go
L   5.24  who was paralyzed-- "I say to you, rise, take up your bed     and go


Mk  2.12  home." And          he rose,         and immediately took up the
M   9.7   home." And          he rose
L   5.25  home." And immediately he rose before them, and              took up that


Mk  2.12  pallet         and went out before them all;  so that
M   9.8                  and went home.                 When the crowds saw it,
L   5.26  on which he lay, and went home, glorifying God. And


Mk  2.12  they were all amazed            and      glorified God,
M   9.8   they were      afraid,          and they glorified God,
L   5.26             amazement seized them all. and they glorified God and were


Mk  2.12            saying, "We never saw anything like this!"
M   9.8                     who had given such authority to men.
L   5.26  filled with awe, saying, "We have  seen strange things today."
```

Example 3. The Sower

```
Mk  4.1   Again          he                    began to  teach   beside the sea.
M   13.1  That same day Jesus went out of the house and sat      beside the sea.


Mk  4.1                  And      a very large crowd  gathered
M   13.2                 And           great crowds gathered
L   8.4                  And when a     great crowd  came together and people
```

33

```
Mk   4.1                                        about him,
M   13.2                                         about him,
L    8.4         from town after town came to    him,


Mk   4.1                   so that he got    into      a   boat and    sat in it on
M   13.2                   so that he got    into      a   boat and    sat there;


Mk   4.2         the sea; and the whole crowd was beside the sea on the land.   And he
M   13.3                  and the whole crowd stood                on the beach. And he
L    8.4                                                                             he


Mk   4.2         taught    them    many things in   parables, and in his teaching he said
M   13.3         told      them    many things in   parables,                       saying:
L    8.4         said                       in a parable:


Mk   4.3,4       to them: "Listen!   A sower went out to sow.        And as he sowed, some
M   13.4                             "A sower went out to sow.        And as he sowed, some
L    8.5                             "A sower went out to sow his seed; and as he sowed, some


Mk   4.4         seed  fell along the path,                          and the birds came
M   13.4         seeds fell along the path,                          and the birds came
L    8.5               fell along the path, and was trodden under foot, and the birds of the


Mk   4.5         and devoured it.    Other seed  fell on    rocky ground, where it    had
M   13.5         and devoured them.  Other seeds fell on    rocky ground, where they had
L    8.6         air devoured it.  And some      fell on the rock;


Mk   4.5         not much soil, and immediately it  sprang up,                since
M   13.5         not much soil, and immediately they sprang up,               since
L    8.6                        and as          it  grew   up, it withered away, because


Mk   4.6         it  had no depth of soil; and when the sun rose it  was scorched, and
M   13.6         they had no depth of soil, but when the sun rose they were scorched; and
L    8.6         it  had no moisture.


Mk   4.7         since it  had no root it  withered away. Other seed  fell among thorns
M   13.7         since they had no root they withered away. Other seeds fell upon  thorns,
L    8.7                                     And some       fell among thorns;


Mk   4.8         and the thorns grew up      and choked it, and it yielded no grain.  And
M   13.7         and the thorns grew up      and choked them.
L    8.8         and the thorns grew with it and choked it.                           And
```

34

```
Mk  4.8    other seeds fell into good soil and brought forth grain, growing up and
M  13.8    Other seeds fell on    good soil and brought forth grain,
L   8.8    some        fell into good soil and                      grew,


Mk  4.8    increasing and yielding   thirtyfold   and  sixtyfold and a hundredfold."
M  13.8                        some a hundredfold, some sixty,   some  thirty.
L   8.8                and yielded   a hundredfold."


Mk  4.9    And he said,              "He who has ears to hear, let him hear."
M  13.9                               He who has ears,         let him hear."
L   8.8    As he said this, he called out, "He who has ears to hear, let him hear."
```

Example 4. The Public Preaching of John

```
M  3.7     But when he saw many of the Pharisees and Sadducees coming for
L  3.7     He said therefore    to the multitudes        that came    out to be


M  3.7     baptism, he said to them, "You brood of vipers! Who warned you to flee
L  3.7     baptized by him,          "You brood of vipers! Who warned you to flee


M  3.8,9   from the wrath to come? Bear fruit  that befits repentance,  and do not
L  3.8     from the wrath to come? Bear fruits that befit  repentance,  and do not


M  3.9     presume to say to yourselves, 'We have        Abraham as our
L  3.8     begin   to say to yourselves, 'We have        Abraham as our


M  3.9     father'; for I tell you, God is able from these stones to raise up
L  3.8     father'; for I tell you, God is able from these stones to raise up


M  3.10    children to Abraham. Even now the axe is laid to the root of the trees;
L  3.9     children to Abraham. Even now the axe is laid to the root of the trees;


M  3.10    every tree therefore that does not bear good fruit is cut down and
L  3.9     every tree therefore that does not bear good fruit is cut down and


M  3.10    thrown into the fire.
L  3.9     thrown into the fire."
```

Example 5. The Beatitudes

```
M  5.3     "Blessed are the poor in spirit, for theirs is the kingdom of heaven.
L  6.20    "Blessed are you poor,           for yours  is the kingdom of God.


M  5.4     "Blessed are those who  mourn,     for they shall be comforted.
L  6.21b   "Blessed are you    that weep now, for you  shall laugh.
```

35

```
M   5.5     "Blessed are the meek, for they shall inherit the earth.


M   5.6     "Blessed are those who  hunger and thirst for righteousness,
L   6.21a   "Blessed are you     that hunger now,


M   5.6         for they shall be satisfied.
L   6.21a       for you  shall be satisfied.


M   5.7     "Blessed are the merciful, for they shall obtain mercy.


M   5.8     "Blessed are the pure in heart, for they shall see God.


M   5.9     "Blessed are the peacemakers, for they shall be called sons of God.


M   5.10    "Blessed are those who are persecuted for righteousness' sake,


M   5.10            for theirs is the kingdom of heaven.


M   5.11    "Blessed are you when men
L   6.22    "Blessed are you when men hate you, and when they exclude you and


M   5.11    revile you and persecute you and utter     all kinds of evil against you
L   6.22    revile you,                and cast out your name as evil,


M   5.12    falsely on my account.             Rejoice            and be
L   6.23            on     account of the Son of man!  Rejoice in that day, and leap


M   5.12        glad, for         your reward is great in heaven, for so
L   6.23    for joy,  for  behold, your reward is great in heaven; for so their


M   5.12    men     persecuted the prophets who were before you.
L   6.23    fathers did     to the prophets.
```

In Luke's Gospel there follow (in vv. 24-26) the Four Woes, corresponding to his Four Beatitudes. The two groups together give the number eight—which is that of the Beatitudes proper of Matt. 5:3-10.

The first result of such a careful study of the Synoptics is the conviction that the three were not produced by completely independent writers. One or two must have written with the knowledge of a third or of a second and a third. The language is too close, up to word-for-word correspondence in places, for independent writers telling the same story. So the Synoptics have a literary interdependence—somehow—that we are certain of. But in just what way—that is the problem. Individual differences of writers will account for the differences. The use of one and/or the other by the second and third—that accounts for the similarities.

The commonly-accepted tradition, Matthew-Mark-Luke, is not the popular explanation for the Synoptic problem today. (The tradition, by the way, was not produced as an early attempt to solve the Synoptic problem at all—it had other roots, whatever these were.) The popular solution of the Synoptic problem today is that which sees two main sources for the present Gospels: Mark's Gospel and a certain source called "Q" (from the German *Quelle*, "source"). Q is really only a shortcut for "what Matthew and Luke have in common apart from Mark."

The arguments advanced for this solution may be briefly summed up. As for Mark, it is held, first, that the order of material where the three Gospels are represented shows Mark to be the source used by the other two, and, second, that the linguistic relations show that both Matthew and Luke have improved the Marcan language, so that Mark must be the original source used by the others. In the case of Q, this assumption is made for the reason that it is easier to see both Matthew and Luke making use of another source altogether than to see either of them using the other. Now, this is a very bald statement of the argument, and the reader will possibly like a little more information and argument, so that bare bones may be clothed with some flesh.

As for the order of the common material in the three Gospels, it is pointed out that, wherever either Matthew or Luke departs from the order of Mark, they differ also from each other; therefore, the basic order is Mark's. This is, however, an invalid argument. The facts of the case can be met just as well by supposing that Matthew was first, that Mark departed from his order at certain spots, and that Luke on the whole stuck to Mark's order with very minor variations. As long as there is one link uniting the other two Gospels, you can explain the changes in order by any arrangement of dependence of one Gospel on another. More and more scholars are losing faith in the argument for Mark's priority based on the order of the common material.

The other argument is far more difficult to present, and it is doubtful whether those without Greek will understand the details in any case. The argument concerns linguistic poorer and better. Some ways of writing are more choice than others: more grammatical, more literary, more adequate, more precise, or even just more interesting. Now, the argument regularly used in connection with the Synoptic problem is that both Matthew and Luke can be shown to be improving Mark's language in one way or another, and it is held that the fact of improvement shows which writer was original. But this very way of putting the argument is derived from the answer held to be true. The relation between Matthew and Mark, to confine ourselves to these two for the sake of the argument, may not be one of *improvement* but one of *impoverishment*. It may be that one writer (Mark) was a poorer writer than the other (Matthew). In that case, if we don't know who was the original writer, we have two possibilities: either that A improved B, or that B produced something worse than A. One action is just as much a possibility as the other. Many scholars write on this matter as if Matthew and Mark were university dons or high school teachers correcting their pupils' efforts at writing. Once this wrong approach is forsaken, we have simply the position just sketched. Now, Mark is on the whole a poor writer, wordy, repetitious, spilling over into wrong grammar and confused constructions. Matthew is much more correct and reliable. So who was first? I hold that you can't demonstrate it from the language both use. Any arguments advanced on the one side to show how Matthew has improved Mark can be matched by arguments on the other side, showing how Mark has changed Matthew for the worse.

Another consideration is of importance in this connection. It is a comparatively easy matter nowadays to copy material from some other source—a book, or pamphlet, or what have you. It would also be easy to make use of such material and make certain changes for the better, if one so desired and if one had the necessary linguistic skill, for the possibility of continual checking and referring back is always there. The situation was quite different with a writer making use of material from a rather clumsy, rolled-up scroll and writing his own material on another clumsy scroll. There would be some gap of time between reading the material to be used and his own act of writing. He would probably read what he was going to use, and then compose more or less freely. The result would be what we see so often: now very close correspondence, now some divergence. If in addition, as is so often the case with Matthew and Mark, there is a big disparity between the length of narratives and accounts, there must be a considerable amount of original composition, no matter who used whom; whether Mark shortened material considerably or whether Matthew expanded at length.

A further argument for the priority of Mark when compared with Matthew is the difficulty of explaining why he should write a Gospel which is so short in comparison with Matthew, and one which leaves out so much of Matthew's most important material. In all questions like this, a most important point to remember is that made years ago by B. H. Streeter: "We cannot possibly know, either all the circumstances of churches, or all the personal idiosyncrasies of writers so far removed from our own time." If we did know these things, we might have an easy explanation for what seems so strange at the moment. Now, let us suppose for a moment that Mark followed Matthew. We might make a guess at his reasons for omitting so much of Matthew. If a writer wanted a fast-moving Gospel with plenty of action and interesting details, and if he felt that Matthew had already supplied a sufficient abundance of Jesus' words, and if he were writing for a Gentile audience, well, we would get something like Mark's Gospel. His stories are full of detail, and almost all the material of interest to Jewish Christians is eliminated. And again, if it is difficult to see how Mark would ignore so much of Matthew, if he were using Matthew, it is equally as difficult to see why Matthew, if he were using Mark, should cut Mark's fine stories into mere snippets.

Other aspects of the two Gospels favour Matthew as being the earlier: the strong Jewish character of the material, which suggests an early stage of the church's existence, and the more developed theological character of the Gospel of St. Mark, which also argues a comparatively early date for Matthew.

We have been concerned with the literary relations between Matthew and Mark. The situation concerning Luke and Mark is different and can be very briefly stated. In their common material Luke is much closer to Mark than Matthew is to Mark; the pattern of differences can be more accurately determined, and that pattern strongly suggests use of Mark by Luke. Luke tells us himself that he made use of various sources (1:1-4), and it seems almost certain that Mark was one of them.

We can be similarly brief in discussing Q. There is no document containing this second source of the popular solution of the Synoptic problem. Q is a reconstruction backwards from the material common to Matthew and Luke. The examples supplied above to show the relationship between Matthew and Luke ("The Public Preaching of John" and "The Beatitudes") show how close the common material can be, but also how far apart. It is not the intention to argue the matter of Q here. It is enough to point out that there are voices being heard nowadays which declare that the hypothesis of Q is unnecessary, and that it is possible to explain the common material as simply a free use of Matthew by Luke. It may also be noted that the hypothesis really does not help very much to explain the problems of the material common to Matthew and Luke. There are three possibilities in relation to Q (if it existed at all): that it was much like Matthew; that it was much like Luke; that it was very different from both. In the first two cases Q does not help at all, and you are in the same boat as you were with Matthew and Luke without supposing a Q. In the third case you now have another difficulty, why both Matthew and Luke changed their original source so differently. Nothing is solved by operating with an unknown source for Matthew and Luke. The only thing you have gained is that nobody can prove you wrong. Neither Matthew nor Luke are likely to rise up from the dead to tell you what really happened. In the resurrection, as C. S. Lewis says somewhere, we will have more important things to talk about.

It should be made clear to those who hold to the inspiration and authority of the Bible, and who may see some kind of irreverent and dangerous treatment of its contents by studies of the kind that have been dealt with in this chapter, that in most cases this fear is mistaken. We may except from this judgment only the wholesale branding of many letters as pseudonymous. Apart from this feature of the literary criticism of the NT, the rest poses no threat to a sound view of the Scriptures. The literature itself presents certain problems, the human mind is curious and would like to find their solution. The actual study of the problems in detail leads to a more complete and adequate grasp and understanding of that sacred literature itself. If God has seen fit to give us His Word in what is truly human language and writing, then the detailed study of that Word in the only form in which we have it must be regarded as an act of genuine reverence for it. Of course, there are many who study the Bible without any of this reverence for it, to whom the books of the Bible are like any other human writings, to be treated with no more and no less consideration and respect. As literary critics they perform the same functions, carry out the same work, as those who acknowledge the divine authority of the Scriptures. It is not at this level of criticism that their critical attitude to the Bible appears very clearly, although on the whole they incline to the more extreme literary-critical positions. The reason why literary criticism does not pose a threat to biblical authority is easy to see. With literary criticism we are, generally speaking, dealing with knowns. The texts are there; the external evidence is available for all. A sane reading of the texts checks exaggerations. These facts set a very definite limit to negative and destructive criticism. It is when we come to speak of form criticism and redaction criticism, where judgments as to what is historically possible, and what is not, are given free play, that we shall meet the critical (used in its very common condemnatory sense) frame of mind in its most distinctive and characteristic form and shape.

CHAPTER THREE
Form Criticism Described

Form criticism takes us to the period before the Gospel writers compiled their works, to the time between the life of Jesus and the writing down of His story, the time say, between the years A.D. 30 and 65. These are crucial years for the tradition concerning Jesus, concerning what He said and did. Written accounts fixed the tradition from the end of that period forward. But what of the previous years? Can we get back to them at all? And if we can, will we not be getting closer in time to the great event itself, with the possibility of arriving at greater certainty as to what really happened?

The beginning of this investigation takes us to the end of World War I. The great names here are all German: Karl Ludwig Schmidt, Martin Dibelius, and Rudolf Bultmann. Schmidt's work (1919) is entitled *Der Rahmen der Geschichte Jesu* ("The Framework of the Story of Jesus"). Much of the Synoptic Gospels is made up of independent episodes with Jesus in the centre. Linking these together, something like the string which unites individual pearls, is in all probability the work of the evangelists. The links are Schmidt's "framework." The framework, it is held, is of great importance in determining the life of the church when the Gospels were written, since it was supplied by the evangelists, but it may be disregarded almost completely when the question of what actually happened is the matter to be investigated.

Dibelius' first work also appeared in 1919, *Die Formgeschichte des Evangeliums* (translated into English in 1934 with the title *From Tradition to Gospel*). He regarded the evangelists as non-literary figures, whose activity consisted of little more than collecting, choosing, grouping, and finally shaping the traditional material. The individual units of the tradition, he held, were formed in connection with missionary preaching and preaching in the course of worship to edify the congregation. Soon the storyteller joined the preacher in producing Gospel material. The actual forms which Dibelius isolated by analysis of the Gospels will be referred to below.

The most famous of the early form critics was Rudolf Bultmann, and he was also the most radical of them. His work, *Die Geschichte der synoptischen Tradition,* was published in 1921. The English translation by John Marsh did not appear until 1963, *The History of the Synoptic Tradition.*

It has just been mentioned that much of the Gospel material consists of rather short, independent, self-contained units. A study of these shows that there are resemblances of formal structure separating one group of these from another. The form critic classifies the various groups he finds, gives them names, and endeavours to reconstruct the history of any piece of tradition from the beginning to its fixing in written state in the Gospels. There are, of course, forms in other sections of the NT also. A hymn, like that of 1 Tim. 3:16 or Rev. 4:11 and 5:9-10, is quite distinct, as distinct as the sonnet with its characteristic 14 lines and metrical scheme, or as distinct as the limerick, known to all. The forms in the Gospels are, however, different from those just mentioned in that they are not literary forms, but forms which emerged spontaneously in early Christian communities. It is believed that the laws which control the passing on of oral traditions can be determined, and that these can then be used to make conclusions concerning the stage which any particular item in the Gospel tradition has reached.

The main form critics classify the forms differently, use their own terminology for the forms they operate with, and also differ as to the number of different forms that can be isolated. In presenting a more complete picture of this whole field of criticism, I propose to make use of the classification of Heinrich Zimmermann *(Die neutestamentliche Methodenlehre*—"New Testament Methodology"). Zimmermann distinguishes, as do most NT scholars, between the tradition of Jesus' words and the tradition of Jesus' deeds. In the tradition of words he distinguished the following forms: prophetic words, wisdom words, law words, parables, I-words, disciples' words. The uniting of words of Jesus into larger paragraphs and compositions, like the Sermon on the Mount, the parable chapter (Mark 4 and its parallels), and Mark 9:33—10:45, is also dealt with in this connection. It seems clear that in this classification form has got mixed up with content. The parable is, plainly, a distinct form, but all the others are distinguished not by form but by what they are about, in other words, by their content.

As for the tradition of deeds we have the following: paradigms, controversy stories, miracle stories, historical tales, and the Passion story. The *paradigm* (Dibelius: also "paradigm"; Bultmann: "apophthegm"; Vincent Taylor: "pronouncement story") is a brief episode, the high point of which is a striking sentence of Jesus, like the call of Levi (Mark 2:14), with the prominent command of Jesus, "Follow

Me." The word of Jesus in such vignettes is of such importance that Bultmann treats these episodes under "The Tradition of the Sayings of Jesus" and not under "The Tradition of the Narrative Material." We have good examples of *controversy stories* in the group of stories in Mark 2:1—3:6. Their characteristics according to Zimmermann are: a question of Jesus' opponents, a counterquestion of Jesus, the answer of the opponents, the final crushing answer of Jesus. *Miracle stories* are simple to detect and are described in similar terms by form critics generally. Most of Dibelius' "legends" are included in Zimmermann's "miracle stories." *Historical tales* contain material not directly concerned with the Christian Gospel, like the death of John the Baptist and the end of King Herod (Acts 12:20-23).

Form criticism, as so far described, may seem to be a harmless activity—and also, I should venture to judge, a pretty useless one as far as most people are concerned. To be informed that this is a miracle story, that a legend, and that again a paradigm will seem to most people as either self-evident or as not of any particular significance and of interest only to those with special literary tastes. However, as we examine the implications of the terms "form criticism" and "form history" (translation of the German technical term for this kind of criticism, *Formgeschichte*), we shall see that its consequences are far more serious than the innocent description would suggest.

As the term "form criticism" implies, the study is used as a historical tool. The proper study of forms, it is held, enables the scholar to make historical judgments as to the origin of the various pieces of Gospel tradition, whether these are narrative or whether they belong to the tradition of words. It is here that the term universally found in connection with form criticism must be taken up for comment: *Sitz im Leben,* seat in life, "the situation or occupation in the life of a community" (Bultmann). The form of the material is linked to its use by the community. As every photograph infallibly points to the standpoint of the one who took it, every form, and every deed or word ascribed to Jesus, points to the situation in which it first saw the light of day and in many cases also to the changes through which it went before its fixing in the written record (form history). That there is a circularity about this method of study is admitted by Bultmann, and it is pointed out frequently by critics of the method. "The forms of the literary traditon must be used to establish the influences operating in the life of the community, and the life of the community must be used to render the forms themselves intelligible" *(The History of the Synoptic Tradition,* p. 5). But then, as Bultmann goes on to assert, this circularity is true of all historical study. We shall return to this matter in the critical section of this chapter, when we subject form criticism itself to critical scrutiny. For the moment it will be necessary to look at a number of examples of form criticism at work; then the nature of the method will become clearer. We shall take up two short sections of St. Mark for this purpose: Mark 2:13-17 and 2:18-20. Comments on the first passage will be culled from various writers; in the second and comparison between the form-critical approach and a conservative historical approach will be instituted.

> Mark 2:13-17: He went out again beside the sea; and all the crowd gathered about him, and he taught them. And as he passed on, he saw Levi the son of Alphaeus sitting at the tax office, and he said to him, "Follow me." And he rose and followed him.
> And as he sat at table in his house, many tax collectors and sinners were sitting with Jesus and his disciples; for there were many who followed him. And the scribes of the Pharisees, when they saw that he was eating with sinners and tax collectors, said to his disciples, "Why does he eat with tax collectors and sinners?" And when Jesus heard it, he said to them, "Those who are well have no need of a physician, but those who are sick; I came not to call the righteous, but sinners."

Heinrich Zimmermann discusses this incident(s) at length in his work. Verse 13 he characterizes as editorial framework which must be separated from the tradition. We are left with two incidents, the call of Levi in v. 14 and the tax collector's banquet in vv. 15-17. The first of the two incidents is a paradigm: it is rounded off, brief, simple; it gives clear prominence to a word of Jesus; and the sequel ("And he rose and followed him") is a model action. So the whole is a pattern of how the Lord calls and also of how the person who hears the call is to act. Where did this incident arise? What is its *Sitz im Leben?* Zimmermann writes as follows: "In the proclamation (sermon) the story is to show by way of an example to those who have come to faith that the call of the Lord makes the believer a disciple with divine authority, and that he (the believer) when called should follow Him with unconditional obedience." This means, in case the reader is still uncertain, that the paradigm was created for this preaching situation and *never actually happened.* The second of the two incidents in vv. 13-17 is classed as a controversy story, and again the *Sitz im Leben* is held to be in the life of the church community, not in the life of Jesus. "The form dates from the time when it was vital to defend the ways of the new community . . . in a technical, scholarly, Pharisaic manner." This story comes from the time when the young church was concerned about defending its action in receiving sinners into its fellowship against critical Pharisees. The modern reader reads the two incidents as one continuous story—but that is only because Mark united what originally were two separate incidents. With Mark the call of v. 14 is only the introduction to the controversy, and the central sentence for him is the word of Jesus in v. 17.

It may be interesting to compare this reading of the whole section with the ideas of other critics. Dennis Nineham, for instance, also holds that two separate incidents have been united into one story, maybe by Mark. As for the genesis of the whole, he seems to agree with those who see in v. 17a ("those who are well . . . but those who are sick") a sentence of Jesus orally preserved in the church without a context, and who believe that vv. 15-17 (without 17a) was supplied by the church as a context for the short sentence, a context made up from well-known habits of Jesus. Lohmeyer in a large commentary on Mark arrives at much the same conclusions. One judgment of his, however, is interesting in itself, and also an indication of the amazing self-confidence of some form critics. He insists that the question of the Pharisees in v. 16 is *impossible* (my emphasis), saying that, since there could be no reason for fellowship between publicans and sinners on the one hand and good Jews on the other, they could not have asked for such a reason. So the question, according to Lohmeyer, is possible only within the congregations of the young church; here is its *Sitz im Leben*.

But form critics do not by any means always agree about their assessment of the same incident—a fact which is of considerable importance when it comes to criticizing the form critics themselves, of which more later. A British form critic, Vincent Taylor, has no difficulty with the pericope we are considering. He says on page 203 of his important commentary on Mark that "much is obscure," that "we do not know when and where the scribes appeared, how they made contact with the disciples," and so on. However, he finds the common reconstruction "unconvincing." He holds that a "narrator uncontrolled by the tradition would hardly have left so many points open," that "the impression left by his narrative is his restraint." "Mark is a writer worthy of trust. He tells what he knows without attempting to answer further questions."

Mark 2:18-20: Now John's disciples and the Pharisees were fasting; and people came and said to him, "Why do John's disciples and the disciples of the Pharisees fast, but your diciples do not fast?"[19] And Jesus said to them, "Can the wedding guests fast while the bridegroom is with them? As long as they have the bridegroom with them, they cannot fast.[20] The

46

days will come, when the bridegroom is taken away from them, and then they will fast in that day."

In the following comparison between a form-critical understanding of this passage and a conservative exegesis of it, I am indebted in very great part to a short study by Dr. Martin Scharlemann in *Affirm*, October 1973.

The form critic (like Nineham) is suspicious of a great deal of this pericope. Verse 18, with its setting of the situation, can easily be explained as a deduction from the rest of the story, since "no connection is established there with what went before in either time or place." Verse 19b looks like a clumsy rehash of 19a, while v. 20 spoils the picture that has preceded, since the bridegroom is not normally taken away from the guests; it looks very much like an allegory of the death of Jesus, which puts us squarely in the period after Jesus' death. So we must look for the *Sitz im Leben* in that post-Easter time. What we have is a pronouncement story or conflict story created by the church to justify the resumption of fasting after Jesus' death, the answer being given authority by the use of Jesus' words in 19a. At the same time it contains a reminiscence that Jesus and His disciples did not fast, unlike the Pharisees and the disciples of John the Baptist.

> In short, the text from Mark consists of four kinds of "stuff." It may include some word from Jesus. It is more likely, however, that most of it comes from the Palestinian period of the church's life. During the course of transmission the item was structured as a pronouncement story, with an opening narrative to provide a setting for the question in verse 19. On top of all that Mark probably added the reference to the bridegroom being "taken away" to relate the passage to Isaiah 53, just as he did in 10:45 (Scharlemann).

The conservative exegete works with the setting given by Mark. He concludes that there was a celebration in the home of Levi. Various possibilities exist for explaining the difficulty set by v. 20. Scharlemann calls to his aid the words of John 14:26, where we have Jesus' promise that the Holy Spirit would call to mind all the things Jesus had told His disciples. This calling to mind he explains as follows:

> Now, it is clear from the four Gospel accounts which we have in our New Testament that this "recalling" on the part of the Spirit was no wooden affair. He did "calling to mind" in such a way as to offer the apostles and the evangelists the words of Jesus in their expanded sense;

that is to say, with the meaning that Jesus intended for the life of the Church through all ages to come. In other words, the exegete will conclude that, if there is really a difference in the "feel" of verses 19b-20 of our text from what has gone before, this change has its source not in the creative imagination of the Church but in that guidance of the Spirit which is known as "inspiration."

An awareness of the phenomenon known as the "expanded sense" of what Jesus said helps the interpreter to appreciate the movement in the life of the Church during the time from Jesus' resurrection to the moment when Mark wrote the first of the four Gospels we now have.

As for the meaning of the incident, Scharlemann sees a number of significances: Even John's disciples and the Pharisees are invited to join in the celebration of the Messianic age; Jesus' claim to be the Messiah is underlined; Jesus is the bridegroom of OT prophecy; the time of fulfilment came with Him, but it involved the necessity of being "taken away," for Good Friday had to precede Easter.

For my own part, I favour a simpler view of the text: that it declares fasting to be incompatible with the time of the bridegroom, Jesus Himself; that v. 20 is a deliberate hint by Jesus of His death in Jerusalem; that, when that happens, His disciples may fast for that brief period. Such a premonition of, and prophecy of, His death does not seem beyond Him of whom we Christians say that He is true man and true God, our Lord. The incompatibility of fasting as a sign of the Old Covenant and the life of the Messianic kingdom is taken up in the sentences about the coat and the patch and the wineskins that follow directly upon this section; and this in turn is the starting point and the authority for the developed teaching of St. Paul on the relation of Law and Gospel in Galatians.

One of the parables treated by C. H. Dodd in *The Parables of the Kingdom* furnishes a nice example of *form history (Formgeschichte)*. He entitles it the Parable of the Money in Trust. Of this parable we have two versions in our Gospels, the Parable of the Talents in Matt. 25 and the Parable of the Pounds in Luke 19. Dodd compares these two versions carefully; all special characteristics of both versions are pruned away, including the special applications suggested by the contexts in which they are found and the introductory sentence of St. Luke—for these developments of the story the evangelists are responsible. One common feature is likewise judged to be a later development of the original parable as told by Jesus. This is the sentence: "To everyone who has will more be given, and he will have abundance; but from him who has not, even what he has will be taken away" (Matt. 25:29). There is a slightly different wording of this in Luke 19:26. Now it so happens that substantially the same sentence is also found in Mark 4:25 in another connection. It is judged that this maxim was not original with the parable, since "there was a tendency to turn sayings of Jesus which were uttered in reference to a particular situation into general maxims for the guidance of the church." So, by playing off Matthew against Luke and both against Mark, Dodd has finally reached the parable as it was in essence spoken by Jesus. Here it is:

> A man called his servants and gave them sums of money in trust, and went away. Later he returned and called them to account. Two of them had largely increased their capital and were commended. A third confessed that he had been afraid to risk his master's money, and had carefully hoarded it: he now restored the precise sum he had received. It is implied that he expected to be commended for his caution and strict honesty. The master however retorted (and here the agreement between the two versions is at its maximum): "Wicked slave! You knew me for a man to drive a hard bargain. You ought to have invested my capital, and then I should have got it back with interest." The third servant is thereupon deprived of his money, which is given to his more enterprising colleague. There the story ended, so far as we can reconstruct the earlier version.

If we now work in the opposite direction, we have the history of the tradition of this parable. First, there is the story as told by Jesus, that is, Dodd's reconstructed version. The second stage is the parable with the addition of the maxim of Mark 4:25. Finally, we have the parable in the two elaborated versions of Matthew and Luke, who add their own eschatological emphasis and other admonitory ideas as well. Matthew, for instance, points to the inequality of gifts apportioned to Christians by giving the three servants in his parable different sums of money.

A question which will naturally suggest itself to readers at this point concerns the effect of form-critical investigations and conclusions on the "life of Christ." What is left of the traditional picture? What can be known for certain about Jesus, what He did and what He said? If we are to judge by the accounts, "lives," written by various well-known scholars, then the answer is: Not much. Let us take up the little book *Jesus*, by Hans Conzelmann. This is actually the English translation, with some additional material in footnotes, of the author's article bearing this name in the prestigious encyclopedia known as *Religion in Geschichte und Gegenwart* ("Religion in History and at the Present"), 3rd ed.

49

What we know of the actual course of Jesus' *life*, according to Conzelmann, is this: Jesus was born of Jewish parents in Galilee. The name of His mother was Mary, and He had brothers and sisters. Jesus was originally a carpenter. He made His first appearance in Galilee. He emerged out of the movement around John the Baptist, but the account of Jesus' baptism by John is legendary (although the baptism may have been a fact). Jesus gathered about Him a circle of adherents of His own, but He did not look forward to a time after His death when these would form a community; His future glance ended with the imminent kingdom of God. All the titles which attempt to describe Jesus and give expression to His self-consciousness: Son of Man, Son of God, Servant of God, Christ (Messiah), were all given to Him by the faith of the church. His ministry was that of miracle-worker and teacher, these two to be understood as a unity. As for the end of Jesus, we can let Conzelmann speak for himself:

> In any case, it is more certain that Jesus went to Jerusalem in order to place before people in their very centre, at the place of the temple and of the highest authorities, a final decision. Naturally his appearance must have been interpreted by the leadership of the people as an attack on the foundations of religion and the nation. So, just as it is narrated, they seized him with the aid of one of the disciples (Judas Iscariot) and handed him over to the Roman procurator, Pontius Pilate, who at that particular time was residing in the city. It is established that Jesus was executed by the Romans (and not by the Jews) since crucifixion is a Roman form of capital punishment and not a Jewish one.

But the story of the entry into Jerusalem is "legend with epiphany motifs"; the report of the institution of the Lord's Supper " in its present form is a cult legend . . . of the celebration of the Christian sacrament"; and as for the trial before the Sanhedrin, "the church shaped the course of events as it conceived them." There is much discussion concerning the resurrection of Jesus, but the upshot of it all is that "the resurrection is not a historical event," that "theology can postulate no historical facts and does not need to do so, since it lives by proclamation." In a word, there is no objective resurrection to be proclaimed as a fact before and apart from faith; only faith believes a resurrection.

Conzelmann takes a pretty radical position, that of Bultmann, who accepts only 2 of some 20 apophthegms (paradigms) as having historical value for Jesus' life, and about 30 individual sayings, 16 maxims, and 12 apocalyptic sayings. Conzelmann distinctly supports Bultmann's position concerning the theological importance of the historical facts about Jesus. He writes: "The single historical fixed point is in fact the naked 'that' *(dass)* of the existence *(Dagewesensein)* of Jesus." He refers here to a famous sentence of Bultmann uttered in 1959, "that only the *dass* matters and is accessible [the fact *that* Jesus existed], not the *was* [*what* He was like]." Radical though the position is, it is not uncommon among form critics. Guenther Bornkamm in his *Jesus of Nazareth* does not finally come up with much more in the way of historical fact, although he does take a more positive stance in respect to the resurrection: "But it is just as certain that the appearances of the risen Christ and the word of his witnesses have in the first place given rise to this faith."

We turn to a common form-critical picture of what Jesus *taught.* For this I am using the material found in Bultmann's *Theology of the New Testament.* To Bultmann, Jesus' message is not part of NT theology but really only a "presupposition" for it. First of all, Jesus was a prophet with a message concerning the reign of God. With this message Jesus is "in the historical context of Jewish expectations about the end of the world and God's new future." However, He significantly reduces the detail of the apocalyptic picture of the future, and introduces something quite new, the quite certain message: "Now the time is come! God's reign is breaking in! The end is here!" Of this dawning kingdom of God Jesus is Himself the sign. "He in his own person signifies the demand for decision." He calls all to be ready for God's demand as He Himself is.

Jesus' proclamation of the demand, the will of God, involves first of all a protest against Jewish legalism. It is, positively, a call to man to love without reservation. The preaching of the dawning of the kingdom of God and the proclamation of the will of God form a unity, which may be thus stated: "Fulfilment of God's will is the condition for participation in the salvation of His Reign." In view of the actual state of the nation, its leaders and the people too in great part, in view of the ritualism everywhere, in view of the love of self and the world, Jesus' message becomes a "cry of woe and repentance." Jesus' teaching concerning God does not differ essentially from that of the OT, so Bultmann holds, but a new note was struck for the Israel of Jesus' time in that Jesus made God a God at hand, who hears and understands, who is Father to His children. This God is a God of forgiveness, who meets man in "his own little history, his everyday life with its daily gift and demand." Of Messianic consciousness Jesus had none. His life and work were not Messianic. What happened was that "the gospel account of his ministry was cast in the light of messianic faith." Which means, in case the strange terminology deceives, that the church, the evangelists, wrote their own convictions, their own faith concerning Jesus, into the story of Jesus. They represented Jesus, His life, work, and teaching, as being what they had come to believe Him to be. But, in doing this, they conveyed a wrong view of the life and teaching of Jesus.

It is at this point that we can take up the critical study known as redaction criticism. For our present purpose it is convenient to treat redaction criticism as a part of form criticism rather than to treat it for itself. Redaction criticism is that aspect of criticism which is concerned with the redactors or editors (the Gospel writers, in a word) of the tradition. From one point of view, this activity is quite different from form criticism. Form criticism is concerned specifically with the individual pieces of the tradition, the different words of Jesus, the varying forms of stories concerning what He or those associated with Him did. Redaction criticism, on the other hand, is concerned with the writers' treatment of what was handed down to them, with their purpose in writing, with their theology, with the ends and goals they intended to gain by their work as a whole. But from another point of view redaction criticisim is a logical development of form criticism. In fact, it presupposes form criticism and the position reached by the form critics. Every commentary you can take up on the various Gospels will deal with the purpose of the writer, the theology he manifests, the peculiar view he has of the Gospel of Jesus Christ. But all pre-form-critical activities in this direction and all attempts to present the purpose of the writer which neglect or ignore form-critical studies cannot be described as redaction criticism. Redaction criticism, to put it another way, is concerned with the final *Sitz im Leben* of the Gospel material, the *Sitz im Leben* of the writer, the editor, the evangelist.

How does the redaction critic get at the purpose of the individual evangelists? In the case of Matthew and Luke, his job is comparatively simple. He believes they both have used Mark's Gospel. So the new material they introduce, the changes they make in what they found in Mark—these together reveal the workings of their minds. They supply hints which can be followed up to lay bare their theology or, perhaps, the theology of the churches where they were active. With Mark, the earliest of the evangelists, the task is far more difficult. For here the critic must first of all separate, from the one web of material, tradition and Mark's treatment of it. But this is not a difficulty at which your redactional critic boggles; it is rather a challenge to his perception and ingenuity. If he is very doubtful about what Jesus said and did, he usually shows no such hesitation about distinguishing between what Mark had in mind and what was handed down to him by tradition.

As has been the case before in this study, examples show best what the critic does. The first example comes from Willi Marxsen, *Mark the Evangelist: Studies on the Redaction History of the Gospel*. The original work was of course in German. The book consists of four redactional studies, and it is his study of the geographical outline which furnishes our example.

One of the most obvious features about the outline of the Gospel According to St. Mark is that the Passion narrative centered in Jerusalem is preceded by a largish slab of material centred in Galilee. Mark, in doing this, conveys the impression that Jesus had never been in Jerusalem before His journey there at the end of His life. Marxsen holds that there are two possible explanations for this state of affairs and writes:

> One is that he constructs it for historical purposes but cannot achieve his goal, due to his ignorance of the territory or to the incompleteness of his materials. In that case, the historical question is disposed of, since it led to the result that Mark was in error. The other explanation is that with his outline Mark has in mind a purpose other than the historical and uses the geographical data to express it.

In his investigation of that purpose Marxsen studies carefully the places where the term "Galilee" appears, and comes to the conclusion that in all these places Mark has inserted the term. It is not good enough in explanation of this fact, Marxsen holds, to say that Mark does this because he is giving us historically trustworthy information. He must have had some other point in mind to fix on the area of Galilee so categorically. Marxsen confidently asserts the answer here: Galilee had some special significance for the primitive Christian community of Mark's day. Just what that special significance was, of course, he can only guess at. He says, "It is conceivable that, for some reason, still to be ascertained, the primitive community was directed to Galilee and assembled there." Marxsen tries to track down this reason. He makes much use of two texts, Mark 14:28 and 16:7, in both of which the disciples are directed to go to Galilee, Jesus being the speaker in the first passage, the angel at the tomb the speaker in the second. However, according to Marxsen, it is really Mark who is responsible for this addition to the tradition. And Mark, for his part, did not think of an appearance of the risen Jesus here, but of His return at the end of the age, the so-called *parousia*. And that in turn is why there is so much emphasis on Galilee in Mark's Gospel; the term "Galilee" becomes an editorial device to bring together the isolated and disparate units of tradition. For Mark "Galilee" is not primarily of historical importance (as the actual place of Jesus' past activity), but rather of theological importance (as the place of the imminent *parousia*). Marxsen tries to pinpoint the actual time when all this might have been possible, and suggests the time about A.D. 66, at the beginning of the Jewish war with Rome, when the primitive community had to flee from Jerusalem to Pella. "This exodus," he argues, "would not only have been related to the political events, but to a heightened expectation of the Parousia as well."

I do not think it amiss to anticipate the critical chapter to follow by pointing out two things: (1) how amazingly different the Gospel of Mark appears to a form or redactional critic and to the normal reader; and (2) how close redaction criticism is to form criticism, or how consistent it is to develop this sort of theological Gospel once it has been decided that most of the units of our Gospel material have been invented by the early Christian communities. If the individual items are a product of the early Christian community, why should not the completed Gospel of an early Christian show the same amount of creative invention?

A second example comes from Norman Perrin, *What Is Redaction Criticism?* It concerns the section Mark 8:27—9:1. To the simple, unsuspecting and unsuspicious reader, this section seems simple enough. Jesus asks Peter who He is, and Peter acknowledges Him to be the Christ. Thereupon Jesus enjoins silence about this on His disciples. His instruction to them that He must die and rise again is met by remonstrance on the part of Peter. Jesus rebukes him and goes on to describe the life of His disciples as a taking up of the cross, as a losing of one's life in order to save it. The conclusion is a warning against being ashamed of Jesus (the cross with its shame is in the background) and a promise that some of those listening to Him would see the kingdom of God come with power.

But this is not what the redaction critic sees in the paragraph. Perrin hardly gives any consideration to this incident as something that happened at a certain time and place in the life of Jesus of Nazareth and His disciples, including Peter. In describing the work of another scholar, he remarks that it (Best's *The Temptation and the Passion: The Marcan Soteriology*) is "a strange book in that the author combines redaction criticism with the assumption 'that Mark believes that the incident he uses actually happened.'" According to Perrin, what we must see here is Mark's own involvement in a doctrinal dispute in the church with which he was associated. Perrin holds that some in the church were

54

describing Jesus as a godlike hero. Mark saw a wrong development in this view of Jesus. What he wanted was that the church should see Jesus rather as the Suffering Servant of God.

> The conclusion is inevitable: Mark presents a false understanding of Christology on the lips of Peter, a true understanding on the lips of Jesus. But in recognizing this, we are recognizing that the narrative is not concerned with the historical Peter's misunderstanding of the nature of Jesus' messiahship but with a false understanding of Christology prevalent in the church for which Mark is writing, i.e. with the heresy that necessitated Mark's Gospel.

It must be emphasized that Perrin is not at all concerned whether anything like what the paragraph seems to say *actually happened* in the lifetime of Jesus.

> It is perhaps not out of place to add that the validity of the Marcan presentation is not dependent upon whether Caesarea Philippi "actually happened" but upon the meaningfulness of the cross as presented to Christian devotion in this way.

In short, what we have in Mark 8:27—9:1 is an allegory, and the biographical framework, the surface appearance, is not to be taken seriously, even if some words actually spoken by Jesus are made use of.

> The characters in the pericope bear names and designations derived from the circumstances of the ministry (Jesus, Peter, the multitude); they also equally represent the circumstances of the early church: *Jesus* is the Lord addressing His church, *Peter* represents fallible believers who confess correctly yet go on to interpret their confession incorrectly, and the *multitude* is the whole church-membership for whom the general teaching which follows is designed.

It will be seen at once that what the form critic and redaction critic finds in our Gospels, and what the church has for almost 2,000 years seen there, are two almost totally different things. The church has read the Gospels as in the main historically reliable accounts of what Jesus said and did when He lived in Palestine, but the form critic sees there only reliable hints as to what the early Christian communities believed about Jesus, whom they acknowledged as Lord and Christ. The first reaction of the simple Christian when confronted with form-critical thinking and "results" is to say or think, "This is the end of the Christian faith. The Christian religion can't possibly be true if so little is known of Him who is its centre." He probably would find himself hard put to maintain his position in debate with a form critic, but there is no doubt that his heart is in the right place and, more, that his "gut" reaction is actually in keeping with the facts of the case. He will find eminent Christians who will put his feelings into telling arguments. I wish to refer to two of these men at this point. The first is E. L. Mascall, professor of historical theology at the University of London. The fifth of his essays in his very readable book, *The Secularisation of Christianity,* is devoted to "Fact and the Gospels," and near the beginning of the essay he has this to say:

> There seems, in fact, to be a deeply rooted tendency in the minds of many biblical theologians to approach their subject in a mood of quite exaggerated scepticism. This may be due to a laudable desire to attract the outsider to the Church by persuading him that it is possible to be a Christian on the basis of a much smaller body of reliable factual material than has generally been supposed to be necessary; I suspect that the usual reaction is a decision that if the factual basis of Christianity is so limited and precarious he might just as well stay where he is, and a suspicion [a nasty smack this! HPH]—no doubt quite unjustified—that the biblical theologians would themselves abandon the formal profession of Christianity if they had not a vested interest in its propagation.

If I may intrude a personal comment here before citing my next witness, I shall say that I have no special interest in believing what the early Christians believed, *if the grounds of their faith are actually unreliable.* If Jesus is Lord only to their faith, but not in and for Himself whether they believed it or not, then He certainly is not Lord for me, any more than the Buddha is my final guide and teacher.

C. S. Lewis is the second witness. Everyone should read his essay, "Modern Theology and Biblical Criticism" in the posthumous collection of essays entitled *Christian Reflections.* The last sentences are the pertinent ones here.

> Once the layman was anxious to hide the fact that he believed so much less than the Vicar: he now tends to hide the fact that he believes so much more. Missionary to the priests of one's own church is an embarrassing role; though I have a horrid feeling that if such mission work is not soon undertaken the future history of the Church of England is likely to be short.

The future history of the church as a whole is likely to be short if the form-critical picture of the historical Jesus takes over. The historical Christian faith of the great creeds and confessions is undoubtedly tied up with the traditional picture of the Gospels as reliable witnesses to Jesus of Nazareth, who was crucified and rose again on the third day. This need not be argued more at this time. Part of the defence of the faith against form-critical corrosion is a critical examination of form-critical principles. And to this we now turn.

CHAPTER FOUR
Form Criticism Criticized

It seems best to begin with some critical observations on the method of form criticism itself. Take the matter of forms. These are said to constitute a historical tool. But what of real value, historically, is gained by saying that this incident is a pronouncement story, that a legend? The historical truth may be couched in all sorts of forms. I can say the same thing in a letter, essay, poem, history book, or magazine editorial. Form and content can in great part be separated. And as a matter of fact, form critics, as far as I can see, don't actually make much use of the distinction of form in arriving at their assessment of the historical value of a certain incident or sentence. In fixing the *Sitz im Leben,* where the real historical judgment is made, the critics' appeal is always to what the content seems to them to suggest. When Lohmeyer says, for example, that the short parables about the garment and the patch and the wineskins cannot refer to a superseding of the Law by the Gospel, "because Jesus could never have got such an idea into His head," it is surely plain that judgment is being determined by what Lohmeyer thinks is historically possible or probable, by what he thinks Jesus could or could not have said, and not at all by the form of the sentences.

A sentence of R. H. Lightfoot is reported which points to the important criticism to be raised against the endeavour to fix the *Sitz im Leben:* "If only they [NT scholars] would say 'we do not know.'" An important work on the criticism of the Gospels has been written by Humphrey Palmer, *The Logic of Gospel Criticism.* He is not a NT scholar; he is a logician who has examined the basic principles of NT critics, especially the adequacy of these principles to produce the results with which we are presented. His conclusion concerning form criticism runs as follows:

> Attempts to classify Gospel paragraphs into distinct literary "forms" are the topic of the present chapter. To affect our grading of these paragraphs as historical evidence, such a classification would need to be dove-tailed with *independent* knowledge of groups·producing, preserving, or altering stories cast in another "form". We have no such knowledge.

And again:

> These conclusions are primarily concerned with the methods and arguments available to biblical historians. Application of these conclusions has here been made only to the extent of remarking that certain inferences require certain sorts of evidence which, in some cases (as in form criticism), do not appear to be available.

It was pointed out early in this chapter that form critics themselves acknowledge that fixing the *Sitz im Leben* of Gospel material involves an argument in a circle; however, the defence of Bultmann was that all historical study works with such a circular argument. What is not made clear in Bultmann's comparison is the big difference that exists in the various historical periods. The quantity of material available concerning Luther, for instance, is so extensive that there is really no danger of arguing in a circle. Each bit of evidence can be checked against a large body of evidence for the period. This is not the situation in respect of the NT Gospels. There is no large body of contemporary material against which their claims can be checked. We know almost next to nothing about the early Christian communities apart from that which appears in the NT itself. An important NT scholar, Miss Morna D. Hooker (*The Son of Man in Mark*, 1967, and other writings) in an essay "On Using the Wrong Tool" (*Theology*, November 1972) says:

> We have no independent knowledge of the groups which formed the pericopes which we are discussing, and we can only deduce the needs and interests of the community which shaped the material from that material itself.

The comparison, in other words, with other historical areas is quite misleading for the reason just mentioned.

Where we don't know, we can only guess, and the fixing of the *Sitz im Leben* for the various paragraphs of Gospel material by NT scholars is just that, guessing, and, as Miss Hooker says again, "sometimes one feels that the hypotheses demonstrate an excessive endowment of imaginative ability on the part of those who put them forward." It should be evident that, the less solid historical evidence there is available for a certain period, the more the refusal to say, "We don't know" opens the gates for subjective judgments and personal feelings of all kinds. The excessive scepticism referred to by Mascall in the quotation above has no historical basis, it is a personal choice of the critics; and if there is any basis for that scepticism apart from personal choice, it lies not in historical factors but in scientifico-dogmatical factors, as will be made clear in the final chapter.

To round out the picture we have tried to draw of the inadequacy of form criticism as a *method* of NT criticism, we may draw attention very briefly to the short period of time when all this church activity was going on before the fixing of the tradition in writing. If we accept April of the year 30 as the time of Jesus' crucifixion, there is no more than 35 years till the writing of the Gospel of St. Mark. For most or all of this period companions, friends, and associates of Jesus were still living. They had memories of what had happened, a living memory which would act as a very strong control on invention and on passing off as words and deeds of Jesus things that never happened and things that were never said. Parallels drawn from folklore and folk tales, and changes in the oral transmission of such material, are of little value just because of this big difference in the time-periods involved.

Finally, on this point we may point out that form critics are not at all agreed in their assessment of the Gospel paragraphs. Take, for example, the little scene of Mark 1:16-20, the calling of the first apostles, Simon Peter and Andrew, James and John. Bultmann and Dibelius call this a biographical apophthegm, presenting an ideal scene, invented from the metaphor about fishers of men. Lohmeyer sees in it an epiphany story belonging to a cycle which told of the appearing of Jesus as the Son of Man. Vincent Taylor comments: "It is astonishing how widely appraisals of the story can differ," and gives his own opinion that there is good reason to describe it as a Petrine story, that is, a narrative which rests ultimately upon a reminiscence of Peter. It is surely clear that a method which results in such divergent opinions is no reliable historical tool. Miss Hooker observes neatly in the previously mentioned essay:

> Of course, NT scholars recognize the inadequacy of their tools; when different people look at one passage and all get different answers, the inadequacy is obvious, even to NT scholars!

We turn from criticism of the method to a criticism of some favourite *assumptions* of form-critical scholars.

The first of these assumptions is repeated again and again by every form critic, often without any attempt at modification, so that it must be regarded as axiomatic for them. One example, from Guenther Bornkamm's famous life of Jesus, *Jesus of Nazareth*, will serve as a sample of the rest.

Although their relation [i.e., that of the Synoptic Gospels] to history is a different one from that of John, they none the less unite to a remarkable degree both record of Jesus Christ and witness to him, testimony of the Church's faith in him and narration of his history.

Both should be continually distinguished in the understanding of the Gospels and in each individual part of their tradition; on the other hand, both are so closely interwoven that it is often exceedingly hard to say where one ends and the other begins. . . . We possess no single word of Jesus and no single story of Jesus, no matter how incontestably genuine they may be, which do not contain at the same time the confession of the believing congregation or at least are embedded therein. This makes the search after the bare fact of history difficult and to a large extent futile.

Now, no matter how often and how strongly the claim is raised that we cannot get at the true facts of the case because they are so closely linked with the faith and witness of the early Christians, there is no reason at all why one and the same man in one and the same declaration should not witness to his faith as well as the facts upon which that faith is based. Just as there is no reason why one, in fighting for his life in a court of law where he is on trial for murder, should not bring together in one defence the strictest speaking of the true facts of the case and the most impassioned plea for his own life. Everyone admits the fact that strong personal concerns and involvement can lead to a distortion of the truth, to a certain emphasis which gives a wrong picture of what actually happened. But it is also true that *personal involvement does not have to have this effect.* In short, we have in the idea that the witness of faith cannot be historical one of those false oppositions (like: not black, but square) which pervert thought and logic, and truth as well.

Another frequent assumption of the form critics is that the early Christians were almost wholly devoid of even elementary historical sense and judgment, in spite of the fact that there were intelligent and educated men among them, like St. Paul for instance. This supposed lack of historical sense comes out in these words from Bornkamm's book mentioned before.

The history of the tradition shows that frequently not only the words of Jesus spoken while he was here on earth . . . soon took on a post-Easter form. For words spoken by the Risen Christ also became words of the earthly Jesus. In principle this is the same process. We have to reckon with it wherever circumstances and questions of the later Church are presupposed in a saying coming from the tradition. . . . Such sayings will originally have been declared to the Church by her inspired prophets and preachers.

An analogous situation would be to declare that I could not tell the difference between a text of the Scripture which I use freely in preaching and a sentence of my own which I make up in the course of a sermon. The only difference would be that the Scripture text is there in writing; the words of Jesus before the written stage, however, circulated orally. I can't believe that this must have been the case so generally as to become the rule just described by Bornkamm. As a matter of fact, there is no proof that this confusion of words ascribed to Jesus and those produced by inspired men of the church ever took place; it is a matter of Bornkamm's say-so.

Whatever evidence exists of this situation actually points in the opposite direction, namely, that men of the church were quite capable of distinguishing between words of Jesus and their own words, even their own inspired words, where "inspired" means approximately words of superior or excellent character. In 1 Cor. 7 Paul on three occasions distinguished between his own advice and commands or advice of the Lord, where he has reported sayings of Jesus in mind (see vv. 10, 12, 25). In Acts 20:35 we have a similar quoting of a word of Jesus (not found in our Gospels, by the way): "remembering the words of the Lord Jesus, how he said, 'It is more blessed to give than to receive.'"

Support for this argument against the customary contention is found in certain facts concerning the use of the phrase "Son of Man." To all intents and purposes, this is a phrase used only by Jesus when referring to Himself. The writers of the NT never refer to Him as "Son of Man." The phrase is treated like a taboo. Now, I know that for all sorts of reasons it is held that the phrase was never used by Jesus of Himself—other positions are taken as well—but the appearances all go the other way: that this was so characteristic a self-designation of Jesus that the Christians, as if by a conspiracy, refused to use it of Him. If this is the true view of the situation, well, the early Christians were very capable of separating the earthly Jesus and what He said from what they themselves or their inspired prophets and teachers said under the influence of the Spirit of the Lord. They could distinguish between what happened before Easter and what happened after it.

A third assumption of the form critics is that the bulk of what makes up the Synoptic Gospels was produced by the early Christian communities. Knowing, as we do, the incapacity of groups of people, whatever the group is, to be really creative, productive of what is fresh, living, dynamic, it certainly is incredible that in this instance so much of spiritual perception and excellence should suddenly have appeared in these early Christian congregations, or that so many spiritually-creative men should have appeared about the same time. When we think of a work like St. John's Gospel or the letters of St. Paul, or of the great literary men of history for that matter, then it is far easier to trace the Synoptic material back to one creative genius than to a whole galaxy of them. A group of people like a Christian congregation or a number of congregations would be still less likely to produce this material. The production of one story like that of the temptation of Jesus would be quite beyond their capabilities. Stephen Neill, in a very excellent book which can be very highly recommended, *The Interpretation of the New Testament 1861—1961*, puts it this way:

> There is a vast difference between . . . the creative working of the community on existing traditions and the idea that the community simply invented and read back into the life of Jesus things that he had never done, and words that he had never said. When carried to its extreme, this method suggests that the anonymous community had far greater creative power than the Jesus of Nazareth, faith in whom had called the community into being.

A final assumption I shall mention very briefly. The form critics insist very dogmatically that the Gospels are not biographical, because the early church had no interest in the historical Jesus. The confidence with which this judgment is stated is matched only by the complete lack of proof that the case was as stated. It is not even probable that the early church would really have been so indifferent to the earthly Jesus, even if they were convinced that the exalted Lord was among them. It is no proof of the form-critical position to refer to the letters of St. Paul and their lack of references to the life of Jesus. From Paul's silence here nothing can be deduced. One can only surmise that if the purpose behind his various letters had demanded it, he would have made references to various aspects of the life of the earthly Jesus. The first verses of St. Luke's Gospel suggest—the very opposite of the form-critical contention—that the early Christians were anxious to "know the truth concerning the things of which they had been informed," and that Luke himself was interested enough to "follow all things closely for some time" (Luke 1:3-4). The First Epistle of St. John was actually written to demonstrate that it was heresy to deny that Jesus had come in the flesh (see 1 John 2:22; 4:2-3; and also 2 John 7).

It is of considerable comfort to the followers of the traditional understanding of the Gospels to know that there is a whole school of scholars which is quite critical of the specific form-critical approach. I am referring to certain Scandinavians who have a quite different explanation of the origin of the Gospel material. One of them, H. Riesenfeld, wrote in an essay in 1960:

> We have attempted to give an answer to the question as to the origin of the Gospel tradition. We must seek its origin ultimately in Jesus and His Messianic self-consciousness. Jesus is not only the object of a later faith, which on its side gave rise to the growth of oral and also written tradition, but, as Messiah and teacher, Jesus is the object and subject of a tradition of authoritative and holy words *which he himself created and entrusted to his disciples for its later transmission in the epoch between his death and the parousia.*

The italics are mine, and these words draw attention to a position which is in all important aspects what Christians have believed for almost 2,000 years, and which is about as far removed from the position of form criticism as can be imagined.

In fact, form criticism is a real novelty in Biblical or NT study, and must meet a very strong challenge as to its credibility by that very fact. An incident quoted in a footnote of C. S. Lewis's essay mentioned earlier highlights this fact most effectively. The footnote reads:

> While the Bishop was out of the room, Lewis read "The Sign at Cana" in Alec Vidler's *Windsor Sermons* (S. C. M. Press, 1958). The Bishop recalls that when he asked him what he thought about it, Lewis "expressed" himself very freely about the sermon and said that he thought that it was quite incredible that we should have had to wait nearly 2,000 years to be told by a theologian called Vidler that what the Church has always regarded as a miracle was, in fact, a parable!

Lewis's remark is even more applicable to the examples we have given of form criticism and redaction criticism. Some sort of case may be made out for Vidler's treatment of the wedding at Cana, for St. John's Gospel is full of symbolism, deliberate symbolism at that, so that the mind of the reader is prepared and even conditioned to look for symbolism all over the place. But this just cannot be said of the other Gospels. On the face of it, the Synoptic Gospels are simple, unsophisticated pieces of writing, as the church has in all its history taken them to be. No one has the right to read this material in a highly sophisticated manner. I should say that the examples from Marxsen and Perrin of the true meaning of "Galilee" and of the section Mark 8:27—9:1 are nothing but pure sensationalism, an arbitrary and even fantastic reading of the writing of simple, even artless, writers. The profundity seen in Mark by Perrin, for instance, stems wholly from Perrin himself. It is simply incredible that

Mark's true intention has been missed all these years till men with the names of Marxsen and Perrin and the rest have suddenly revealed it to us. If one really wants to do away with what the Gospels say when taken at their face value, it would be far more rational simply to reject the material or most of it as wrong and mistaken than to make highly-imaginative and arbitrary guesses as to some abstruse underlying intention of the writers.

It should be made clear that, in the criticism of form criticism that has been developed above, no attempt has been made to belittle the learning of the scholars involved. This is often of quite a prodigious kind. There is only an appeal to common sense and a warning against an inappropriate reading of certain material. The famous Harnack wrote years ago that the "New Testament is such a small book, the fragment of fragments, that one cannot learn from it only the methods of solid historical criticism. . . . Only the knowledge of many writings can give a man that sense of proportion which is needed for solid judgments." And Lewis takes up the idea in a more developed fashion in the essay referred to earlier. He says he distrusts the great biblical scholars "as critics," and goes on to show why:

> They seem to me to lack literary judgment, to be imperceptive about the very quality of the texts they are reading . . . a strange charge to bring against men who have been steeped in those books all their lives. But that might be just the trouble. A man who has spent his youth and manhood in the minute study of New Testament texts and of other people's studies of them, whose literary experience of those texts lacks any standard of comparison such as can only grow from a wide and deep and genial experience of literature in general, is, I should think, very likely to miss the obvious things about them. If he tells me that something in a Gospel is legend or romance, I want to know how many legends and romances he has read . . . not how many years he has spent on that Gospel.

Not everything that has been done in the area of form and redaction criticism is a dead loss. The very fact that so much time and labour is spent on a detailed study of the texts inevitably brings many incidental facts to light which enrich our general knowledge of the Gospels quite considerably. But the very heart of the study must be judged a failure, and its goal, to throw light on the formation of the tradition before that tradition was committed to writing in our Gospels, must be declared to be unattainable by that path.

It may be that Lewis's hope will yet be fulfilled. He "does not expect the present school of theological thought to be everlasting," he writes. "In other fields of study the 'assured results of modern scholarship' are transitory. . . . The confident treatment to which the New Testament is subjected is no longer applied to profane texts."

If anyone present tonight has felt . . . shy and tentative doubts about the great biblical critics, perhaps he need not feel quite certain that they are only his stupidity. They may have a future he little dreams of.

CHAPTER FIVE
Content Criticism
and the Historical-Critical Method

Some years ago I was in discussion with Guenther Bornkamm on a street corner near Moore Theological College, Sydney, New South Wales. We were discussing lectures that had been given by Dennis E. Nineham on the resurrection of Jesus. Nineham had taken the position that the resurrection of Jesus was a story invented by the early Christians to explain their faith in Jesus. This was the first time I had come up against this particular explanation and I was pretty free with my criticism. Bornkamm made an observation, which I take to be the key to a very great deal of modern writing on the NT. He said: "But we cannot get away from our own shadow." That is to say: What is not in keeping with our present world-view cannot be true, and if historical incidents are involved they *cannot* have happened as they are reported to have happened.

Now, your moderns state this conviction with all possible clarity and sharpness. The writers of *Biblical Criticism*, Vol. 3 of "The Pelican Guide to Modern Theology," for example, write concerning the miracle stories of the New Testament:

> . . . in the case of miracles they (the form critics) point to the likeness to stories circulating in both the Jewish and the Hellenistic world of the time when the gospels were being written, and to the pre-suppositions of such stories; these were very often that the illnesses were caused by demons, so that the effectiveness of the story and therefore its truth depends upon belief that Jesus exorcized the demons and so worked his cures. Since we now know that demons are not the causes of diseases we cannot believe the stories; but we can assign a reason for their having been told of Jesus—the desire to enhance his reputation. This desire lay in the minds of the members of the early church (pp. 248—249).

A second example comes from Willi Marxsen's *The Resurrection of Jesus of Nazareth*. His position throughout the writing is that nothing in our experience or our knowledge of reality gives us the right to expect a dead man to rise, and that therefore a factual or physical resurrection could not have occurred. Accordingly he can write: "I said earlier that I could say of a past event that it was a miracle only if I experienced a corresponding miracle today." Again:

> Anyone who says this was not a real event [i.e., the resurrection of Jesus] is therefore saying something different from what these writers thought [i.e., the NT writers]. But is he therefore necessarily wrong? It must be at least admitted that the authors of the texts were expressing *their* view, while the person who says something different is expressing *his*. The two opinions may diverge. But then it must surely be permissible to discuss the question who is right.

It is obvious in this case of conflict where Marxsen stands: He will uphold the modern world-view against the convictions of the NT authors.

Our third example consists of some sentences from a very famous writing of Rudolf Bultmann, the essay which introduced his whole program of demythologization and which first appeared in 1941.

> For all our thinking is shaped for good or ill by modern science. . . . Now that the forces and the laws of nature have been discovered, we can no longer believe in *spirits, whether good or evil*. . . . *Man is essentially a unity*. He bears the sole responsibility for his own feeling, thinking, and willing. . . . Biological man cannot see how a supernatural entity like the *pneuma* (Spirit) can penetrate within the close texture of his natural powers and set to work within him. . . . Again, the biblical doctrine that *death is the punishment of sin* is equally abhorrent to naturalism and idealism, since they both regard death as a simple and necessary process of nature.

An interesting variation on the theme that what cannot have happened according to our view of nature did not happen is the claim that the more likely historical situation is the right and proper historical situation. For an example of this supposedly-historical principle we turn to the writers of the first example just referred to, Robert Davidson and A.R.C. Leaney, authors of *Biblical Criticism*. They contrast the reading of the Gospels by an uncritical reader and the critical scholar. The uncritical reader believes the real situation to be that which the text suggests every time. For instance, in Mark 12:13-17, the Pharisees and Herodians ask Jesus a question about taxes, to which Jesus gives the well-known answer: "Render unto Caesar the things which are Caesar's, and unto God the things which are God's." The simple reader transports himself back to the temple near the end of Jesus' life and sees an attempt by enemies of Jesus to trick Him into making a damaging statement.

The form critic suspects almost everything about the little story. He finds a different situation, in which the main line of the incident might fit better. Members of the early church needed guidance on the problem whether they ought to pay taxes to the Roman Empire in view of their loyalty to God and their belief that the judgment on this world was near at hand. Would payment of taxes be consistent with Christian principles? The story gives the answer YES. "A story was invented which invested a prudent practice with the Lord's authority."

It is necessary, in passing, to point out how the principle we have illustrated in various ways quite demolishes the Christian faith, if indeed the attentive reader has not already drawn that obvious conclusion for himself. Davidson and Leaney are quite frank and open about the results of Biblical criticism upon the content of the ancient creeds. They point with satisfaction to the advantages that accrue once we have come to the point of seeing that we have excellent accounts of the ways the evangelists envisaged Jesus and His career, but that we have no right to say, "This is what actually happened."

> The Jesus who seems to have entered upon a career of self-advertisement, proclaiming in effect, "I am the son of God; therefore anyone who questions my authority will be lost!" is now seen to be a fantasy. . . . We come rather to the conclusion that Jesus may be properly regarded not as a phantasm who came down from heaven to earth and went back again, but as a man of such quality . . .
>
> Other considerations concern Paul: Is there any meaning still to be given to his words when he says of Christ Jesus that "God designed him to be the means of expiating sin by his sacrificial death, effective through faith" (Rom. 3:25)? Or, again, if criticism shows that Jesus did not found a church but sought to reform a community which he already regarded as the people of God, what authority—indeed, what point—is there in the church of today? . . . Can we attach any meaning to the doctrine of the grace of God? . . . Is there any reality corresponding to that in the New Testament expressed in the words, "the Holy Spirit"?

Bultmann's famous essay referred to earlier goes the same way. All the statements of the Apostles' Creed are regarded as mythological, except "He was crucified, dead, and buried." Incarnation, Virgin Birth, Redemption, Resurrection, Descent into Hell, Ascension, Session (sitting) at the right hand of God, the Return to Judgment—these are all myths, like the nature myths of the ancients, together making up the truth presented that the authentic human life is the life that does not look for security but that lives wholly from faith and in love.

It is time to look critically at the historical principle with which we began this chapter: what is not in keeping with our present world-view, our convictions concerning nature and man in it, cannot have happened and did not happen.

We begin with the relation between historical fact and practical possibility. I think we may grant that normally we look for more proof in proportion to the unlikelihood of some event or happening. If I am informed by my wife that some bad boys are raiding my orange tree, I leave my desk at once to deal with the intruders. If, however, she tells me that there are elephants in the back garden, I shall probably not do anything till they actually burst into the house. The logical end of this normal process of reasoning is indeed to be sceptical and unbelieving when what is asserted to have happened is something that neither I nor anybody else has actually experienced. In short, this amounts to support of the principle: what is impossible according to my view of the world is non-historical.

But in making this statement, we must know what we are doing: we are leaving the strictly historical method of determining what happened from the evidence that is there, in order to determine what happened from a prejudice, a prejudgment, a dogmatic position. I should really accept the witness, the evidence, of reliable witnesses if they tell me about marauding boys or erring elephants. I should do this, on strictly historical grounds, even if the witness happens to be *one* reliable person. Not to do so shows the operation of the prejudice based on probabilities and possibilities. What lies behind our normal reaction of non-belief when the humanly impossible is asserted is a philosophy, a world-view, not the principle of historical evidence pure and simple. The position of critical biblical scholars, too, is based on dogma, philosophy, certain scientific prejudices, not on strictly historical arguments.

In that respect the critic is not one whit more scientific, historically, than the non-critical conservative. The latter's non-critical reading of the New Testament is based on the prejudice of the Christian creeds: that miracles did and can happen; that God is almighty and can enter history and the individual tightly-knit human being; that Jesus was and is the pre-existent Son of God, one with the Father, and that this authority was His also in His few years in Palestine; that He did rise from the dead into a new life; that in His reign over all things He sends His Spirit to bring men to salvation; etc. Obviously, once we have granted the presence in history of a truly divine Being, of this new dimension which far transcends the human, then previous impossibilities become possibilities. The whole field of what is possible and what happened, historically speaking, is immensely enlarged. But as just pointed out, the historical critic has his own set of dogmas and prejudices.

So what we see in the debate between conservative and critical biblical scholars are not really different views of history, but different faiths, philosophies, and convictions as to what truth is. We have at bottom a battle between faith and unbelief. Which is not to say that all critical scholars are unbelievers. God alone must judge who are His and who are not. But there can be no doubt that the difference between the fundamental attitudes toward history that have been outlined is that of faith and unbelief. Some words from C. S. Lewis's *Miracles* are decidedly to the point here, words that contain also a call to Christians to "get rid of their own shadows":

> When you turn from the New Testament to modern scholars, remember that you go among them as a sheep among wolves. Naturalistic assumptions . . . will meet you on every side—even from the pens of clergymen. This does not mean . . . that these clergymen are disguised apostates . . . It comes partly from what we may call a "hangover". We all have Naturalism in our bones and even conversion does not at once work the infection out of our system. . . .And in part the procedure of these scholars arises from the feeling which is greatly to their credit. . . .They are anxious to allow to the enemy every advantage he can with any show of fairness claim . . .
>
> In using the books of such people you must therefore be continually on guard. You must develop a nose like a bloodhound for those steps in the argument which depend not on historical and linguistic knowledge but on the concealed assumption that miracles are impossible, improbable, or improper. And this means that you must really re-educate yourself; must work hard and consistently to eradicate from your mind the whole type of thought in which we all have been brought up.

The effect of the conviction that only what is possible according to our modern world-view can be historical is not merely to demolish the traditional faith as such—its worst result. The critic feels in duty bound to put something in the place of what he has torn down. If things did not happen as we are told in the NT they did, what did happen? If there was no resurrection in the sense of the church's confession, then what did take place? And how did the idea of a resurrection arise? Taking the specific instance of the resurrection of Jesus, we have a good example of scholarly (?) reconstruction in Willi Marxsen's *The Resurrection of Jesus of Nazareth,* a work referred to earlier. Here is part of his explanation of what happened.

I said earlier that the experience of being called to faith by Jesus was interpreted with the help of already existing ideas. Let me show in more detail what I mean. Someone discovers in a miraculous way that Jesus evokes faith even after his death. He now asks what makes it possible for him to find faith in this way. The reason is that the Jesus who died is alive. He did not remain among the dead. But if one wanted to claim that a dead person was alive, then the notion of the resurrection of the dead was ready to hand. So one made use of it. In doing so there was no need to pin oneself down to a particular form of this idea; and it is quite possible that different notions were associated with the doctrine in various sections of the primitive church. But the common formula "Jesus is risen" could still be used. Or one could go a stage further in interpretation and say: "God raised Jesus from the dead."

Marxsen finds other phrases in the NT to state the fact that Jesus still works faith today, like the idea of exaltation. Consistently he goes on to declare that, if the primitive church found interpretative phrases like resurrection and exaltation, we have the right to find other phrases for the same purpose, phrases which may be more comprehensible and so more valuable today. He suggests two: "Still he comes today" and "The cause of Jesus continues." Marxsen's actual argument does not concern us—it is very weak and can be shot full of holes. It is mentioned only as one example of what goes on continually in all NT critical work. It is a direct result of the declaration that the miraculous has no historical standing. If we could imagine the NT without the miraculous, then I doubt very much whether any NT scholar would spend one sleepless night inventing substitute situations-in-life for those the Gospels tell us of. It would be a fruitless occupation.

The truth is that it is just not a historical task to invent history to replace the supposedly historical situation you have rejected. If the historian has a number of conflicting accounts of an event or conflicting pictures of some historical character, he can make a choice among them or between them, or he may be able to find some combination which has historical plausibility about it. The historian, for instance, has very different pictures of Socrates in Plato's *Dialogues*, Xenophon's *Memorabilia*, and in Aristotle. He will use his historical skill and perception built up over the years to arrive at a picture of Socrates which seems to fit all the evidence, accepting some evidence outright, rejecting other evidence, and harmonizing accounts where possible. But where he has only one account, one strand of evidence, he can accept it or reject it. He can't make up something to take the place of the evidence he has rejected. Or he *can*; but what results is only an indication of his own ingenuity and cleverness, as a novel is, but it has *no historical validity or standing at all*. This judgment is really the same as that made in a previous chapter concerning the need to keep silent where we do not know, but it has been gained through argument from another point of view.

The scholarly activity we have been describing and criticizing in these chapters is frequently called "the historical-critical method." A consideration of this term and its underlying philosophy can act as a convenient summary of what we have been doing.

The historical-critical method is not always described as clearly and sharply as it might be. The reason for this is not that there *can* be no clear description and definition of it, but the fact that many writers want to have their cake and eat it as well. They do not personally share the basic philosophy or theology of the pure practitioners of the method, but at the same time they would like their work to be recognized as scholarly, an end which can hardly be achieved without tipping the cap to historical criticism. So on occasion we meet descriptions which may leave the reader in uncertainty as to what the historical-critical method really is. However, no one is helped by such a state of affairs. For understanding, we need clear ideas, sharp outlines, as accurate definitions as possible. Such a clear description of the historical-critical method follows, and every reader should be aware that of the many biblical scholars in the world who accept the method none would find fault with this description. It comes from the Introduction (written by R. P. C. Hanson) to the previously-mentioned Vol. 3 of "The Pelican Guide to Modern Theology." This is how the historical-critical method is understood by the present writer, and this is what will be examined critically.

> Only a hundred years ago, most Christians of all traditions would have been quite content to describe the Bible as inerrant, infallible, and inspired equally in every part. . . .But in spite of shocked churchmen . . . the revolution moved inexorably on. It consisted in the simple but far-reaching discovery that the documents of the Bible were *entirely conditioned by the circumstances of the period in which they were produced* [my italics] . . . . It meant that the books of the Bible were henceforth open to being treated precisely as all other ancient documents are treated by historians of the ancient world. No sanctity, no peculiar authority, no special immunity to objective and unsparing investigation according to the most rigorous standards and methods of scholarship, could ever again be permitted to reserve the Bible from the curious eyes of scholars. The Bible might well in future be approached by scholars with

presuppositions about it in their minds, but not the presupposition that this book is a sacrosanct preserve whose historical accuracy and literal truth must be maintained intact.

The historical-critical method as just defined and described is *not* a legitimate, appropriate, relevant method of study for Christian theologians and Christian people. The Christian has a faith, certain convictions about what is truth and what not, which simply cannot be adjusted to or harmonized with the historical-critical method. If he confesses the Apostles' Creed and other more developed creeds in agreement with it, he is committed to a series of statements (of course, not mere statements, but truths of the gravest import) which are just not possible where the historical-critical method is being consistently employed. We have already pointed out that for historical criticism miracles are impossible, that what we have not experienced and what our world-view does not permit cannot have happened. For the critical historian, man, not God, is the authority. The method allows no room whatever for the Word of God. There remains only the subjective judgment, maybe, that such-and-such is Word of God for me. But this also is pure self-deception. What is Word of God for me can never be set forth as Word of God for anyone else. And if I myself, in my own individual person and on that basis alone, decide what is Word of God, then there is no difference between Word of God and my own judgment. Word of God is my own word, and has no more authority. And "God" itself becomes a mere convenient expression for what touches me most deeply. All this puts an unbridgeable gulf between the faith and convictions of the Christian—"Christian" defined in the only legitimate way as one whose faith is that of the church's creeds—and the consistent practitioner of the historical-critical method. No kind of logic or glib talk or prevarication can bring the two together.

However, the judgment just made does not mean that no aspect of the method we are talking about can be of use for the Christian. It is the historical-critical method as such which is impossible for the Christian, the method seen from its innermost being and rationale. But this does not eliminate the possibility that certain aspects of it may have their value, aspects which are peripheral, by the way, accidental, when compared with the heart of the method, but which in themselves are of considerable importance. Some of these may be referred to briefly at this point.

Our knowledge of the language of the NT has been immeasurably increased and made more accurate by the detailed investigation of the

Greek of the NT period. It is plain from these studies that the Greek of the NT is not some heavenly Greek, Greek of the most perfect kind, nor a debased, bastard Greek, but simply the common Greek (Koine) of the period, the Greek which developed over great parts of the eastern Mediterranean as a result of the conquests of Alexander the Great. Writers of the NT differ quite greatly in their use of this Greek, with Mark representing a rather low level of written Koine, Hebrews the opposite extreme. What better medium for the spread of the Gospel than the commonly-spoken language of the time?

The backbreaking, detailed work involved in the study of early written texts has resulted in the situation that we can have extreme confidence in the text of our NT, up to 95 per cent of the whole, an absolutely staggering percentage when we compare it with the situation that prevails in respect to all other ancient Greek and Latin literature.

The literary analysis of our texts, too, has brought us to understand them considerably better, although we shall probably never understand them as well as those who first wrote and read them. Strange, way-out, and radical theories concerning our NT writings are advanced often enough, but the correction of these lies in the writings themselves, to which all have access, and sound common sense soon relegates many of these literary vagaries to limbo.

So also, the close study of religions contemporary with the rise of Christianity is not without advantage for NT studies. After all, the early Christians preached the Gospel to peoples who, apart from the Jews, were all heathen. They had to make the Gospel intelligible to them, show the difference between what they had previously believed and the new thing being proclaimed to them. Some of this conversation or confrontation, naturally, has been transferred to the NT writings, so that they in turn, especially the writings of St. Paul and St. John, become more intelligible when the heathen opponent is better understood. Here, too, there are false developments, as when scholars write as though the Christian religion was hardly more than an amalgam of Jewish and heathen religious ideas. Here, too, correction of a wrong picture is easy, for the NT is there and the documents of the heathen religions as well. No one can be imposed upon who does not want to be.

The same observations, however, cannot be made concerning form criticism and its development in redaction criticism. Here, as has been pointed out, we are no longer dealing with knowns, but with unknowns, in very great part. In this area the baleful effects of a criticism which denies the miraculous become painfully evident. There is no possibility from within the discipline itself to correct developments that destroy the

Christianity of the creeds. The form critic cannot in any absolute way be proved wrong in many of his guesses, but neither can he, by the same token, show that he is right. And if he insists on his "shadow," his conviction, his philosophy, his prejudice that nothing can have happened that we have not experienced, in short that miracles are impossible, then we conservative believers can do nothing else than insist on our faith, our conviction, our prejudice that the Incarnation, the Resurrection, and the other miracles that make up the Christian faith have happened. Or, in other words, as we have pointed out before, different prejudices, different convictions, different faiths make for different conclusions—not different understandings as to what constitutes evidence. The heart of the historical-critical method is a faith, a philosophy, a view of the world and of nature. That philosophy the Christian believer cannot accept. And so, while using those results of historical-critical study that can be liberated from the underlying philosophy, he cannot, and ought not, and will not accept the method in all its parts and with all its presuppositions.

Well, what then will be an acceptable method for him? The simple answer is: a historical method which does not dissolve the foundations of his faith. That method we may call a historical-Biblical method. We can't get away from the element of history; that must be made plain. God has chosen to make Himself known and to carry out His plan of salvation for men in and through history. Once this has happened, even God cannot extricate Himself from the history into which He has placed Himself, that is, from that portion of history in which He has acted uniquely, very particularly, once for all—for our salvation. Historical study must remain, historical investigation as rigorous as we can make it. If possible, the Christian theologian should be even more at home in the pertinent history than the historical critic, for he has more to lose than the historical critic if the history becomes uncertain, doubtful, or even untrue. The historical critic can face any upset of the history without turning a hair. The history is at bottom unimportant for his theology; what counts is the thought, the idea, the abiding truth. He can always end up as an existentialist, a humanist, an atheist, a socialist, or what have you. But the Christian will end up with nothing. If Jesus of Nazareth in His birth, life, and death is not the Christ, the Messiah, the Son of God, then he has no God left whom he knows and whom he can worship. If the Resurrection was no real resurrection but only an early Christian construction, a means of interpreting a certain experience, then, again, the whole Christian faith evaporates, leaving nothing behind but some moral ideas. And these we can find in any case in other

76

religions or in the moral teachings of various philosophers, so that we would not miss very much if even these vestiges of ethics disappeared. The Christian faith is so closely tied up with history, then, because God Himself, so the Christian revelation has it, entered into history for our salvation.

The Christian's attention to history, however, will operate within the limits and controls of the biblical witness, within the controls crystallized in the Christian creeds: that "Jesus Christ came down from heaven for us and for our salvation, and was incarnate by the Holy Spirit of the Virgin Mary, and was made man, and was crucified also for us under Pontius Pilate. He suffered and was buried, and the third day He rose again according to the Scriptures." This is not a scheme arbitrarily imposed upon the historical facts, but the witness of the facts themselves as interpreted by Jesus Himself and handed down to the church through His chosen apostles. This is the Christian faith, and as long as Christians remain here on this earth, Christian theologians will be compelled by their faith to interpret the New Testament historically *and* biblically.

A Brief Bibliography

A. Short Presentations by Supporters of Critical Methods

Beardslee, William A. *Literary Criticism of the New Testament.*

McKnight, Edgar V. *What Is Form Criticism?*

Perrin, Norman. *What Is Redaction Criticism?*

(All in the series "Guides to Biblical Scholarship," published by Fortress Press, Philadelphia.)

B. Discussions by Opponents of Critical Methods

Lewis, C. S. *Miracles.* Collins (Fontana Books).

———, *Christian Reflections* (especially the essay "Modern Theology and Biblical Criticism"). London: Geoffrey Bles, 1967.

Mascall, E. L. *The Secularisation of Christianity* (especially Chapter V). London: Dalton, Longman, and Todd, 1967 (a Libra Book).

Neill, Stephen. *The Interpretation of the New Testament 1861—1961.* Oxford University Press, 1964 (Oxford Paperbacks). Excellent!